The Mothers and Daughters
of the Bible Speak

Also by Shannon Bream

Finding the Bright Side:
The Art of Chasing What Matters

The Women of the Bible Speak:
The Wisdom of 16 Women and Their
Lessons for Today

THE
MOTHERS
AND
DAUGHTERS
OF THE
BIBLE SPEAK

LESSONS ON FAITH
FROM
NINE BIBLICAL FAMILIES

SHANNON BREAM

FOX
NEWS
books

HarperCollins books may be purchased for educational, business, or sales promotional use. For information, please email the Special Markets Department at SPsales@harpercollins.com.

Fox News Books imprint and logo are trademarks of Fox News Network LLC.

FIRST EDITION

Illustrations courtesy of Adobe Stock, Inc.

Library of Congress Cataloging-in-Publication Data has been applied for.

ISBN 978-0-06-322588-6

22 23 24 25 26 LSC   10 9 8 7 6 5 4 3 2 1

For Jouetta:
a mother of selfless devotion, deep faith, abiding joy,
and a little mischief. I'm so grateful I married your son,
so I get to call you "Mom" too.

See, I am doing a new thing!

Now it springs up; do you not perceive it?

I am making a way in the wilderness

and streams in the wasteland.

—ISAIAH 43:19

CONTENTS

CONTENTS

Have you ever had one of those days? A day when it seems like everything that happens gets in the way of your progress and plans? I had one of those in 2021, and the lesson it taught me is at the heart of this book. It can be hard to keep your mind focused on things above when circumstances here on Earth seem to be specifically aimed at stealing your joy, but nothing we encounter in life is without purpose.

It was early morning. I had an event planned for a Saturday evening, hundreds of miles from my home. We had rolled out of bed to get to the airport, boarded, and were ready to go at 7:45 a.m.—a stretch for me as I normally don't get to bed after work until 2:30 a.m. I hadn't done much but throw on some relatively presentable casual clothes after brushing my teeth. That's when the announcements began. "We've got a minor mechanical issue to rectify and then we'll be on our way."

I have a confession to make: I am a closet travel agent. It's not just that I love to actually go places; it's that I want to investigate and research every possible option long before I lock in the plans themselves. So when I heard about the delay, I also began to dig up all the possible options to get us to our event on time. There was another flight leaving for our connecting city very soon, but we'd have to abandon the flight we were on and take our chances that our luggage would make it. We rolled the dice. After several more close calls and irritating delays, we landed safely at our destination.

Time was tight, but I was confident that I could still pull together my hair and makeup and take out my secret weapon: the black dress that does not wrinkle. Speaking of wrinkles, guess what happened when we checked for our baggage? You can see where this is going. Panic began to set in. The only luggage that had made it was the one with my swimwear. I couldn't exactly take the stage in a Miraclesuit and a sarong.

The baggage office at the airport told me there was a "good chance" the missing bags would show up on the next flight coming in from the city we had just connected through. By my calculation I could hit up a local drug store and pull off an emergency makeover, but I might still have to show up on stage in glorified sweats. I was sleep-deprived and beginning to lose it, my worry intensified by the news that the rental car company couldn't find us a vehicle—despite our reservation.

After a thirty-minute delay, we sped off so I could rush through a drugstore, grabbing tinted moisturizer, mascara, blush, dry shampoo for my greasy hair—anything that might help. There was just enough time for us to dash back to the airport to see if the two missing bags were indeed on that incoming flight.

In the first bit of good news that day, they showed up! Pedal to the metal, I started putting on my face in the car. When we arrived at the church, the pastor and his wife could not have been kinder. They had been praying for us all day, through the many unplanned irritations and detours. As I made peace with the slicked-back ponytail I'd be sporting, I threw on that wrinkle-defying dress, and we said a quick prayer.

Before I spoke that night, three women took to the stage and shared deeply personal stories of loss and how God had redeemed their enormous suffering for His glory. With each bit of vulnerability and pain they revealed, I felt a dagger going through my own heart. I had spent the day angry with everyone and everything, insulted that my plans were being thwarted at every turn. I demanded to know why God would drag me through these circumstances when I was exhausted and trying to show up to make Him look good. Oh, and by the way, why wasn't He going to let me look good for this event? A glam session courtesy of Walgreens was not what I had in mind! I mean, if I didn't look good, how was I supposed to make Him look good?!

Ouch. I sat in that pew watching the day flash before my eyes, finally getting the point.

This day wasn't about my getting up on that stage unflustered and polished; it was about realizing that I'd had the wrong focus all day long. This event was about walking through life with women who had suffered loss or were in the midst of it at that very moment. Why did I think that showing up looking as though I had not a care in the world was the right way to share God's grace and promises? I was in tears by the time the pastor's wife introduced me and told the women I'd had such a rough day. All day, all those annoying disappointments were actually the whole point. The Lord took me on that roller coaster so that my heart would be much more attuned to what He wanted to say through me. It wasn't about me; it was about Him and the women He deeply loved. It was about being humbly vulnerable, genuine, and transparent.

So much of what we read in the Scriptures magnifies this same lesson over and over again: the journey *is* part of the process. What looks like a delay in getting to "the good stuff" is an inescapable, necessary leg of the trip. Even Jesus Himself modeled that for us in Matthew 3:13–4:25. At the beginning of the passage we see John the Baptist baptizing Jesus.

As soon as Jesus was baptized, He went up out of the water. At that moment heaven was opened, and He saw the Spirit of God descending like a dove and alighting on him. And a voice from heaven said, "This is my Son, whom I love; with him I am well pleased." (Matthew 3:16–17)

Wow! God Himself spoke from heaven, making clear to everyone that Jesus was indeed His son. Could there be a more perfect time for Jesus to launch into His public ministry? Why not walk straight from that baptism and heavenly proclamation into the streets and start doing miracles?

Because that wasn't the plan. Instead, this is what happened immediately after Jesus was baptized.

Then Jesus was led by the Spirit into the wilderness to be tempted by the devil. After fasting forty days and forty nights, he was hungry. (Matthew 4:1–2)

Before Christ could begin His public ministry, He was sent on a detour that tested all the limits of the human mind and body He'd chosen to take on. In the verses that follow we see the devil repeatedly tempt, test, and taunt Jesus. For weeks, Jesus was alone—hungry and thirsty—and tormented by His enemy, our enemy. At any moment, Jesus could have called the whole thing off. Instead, He stood firm, quoting Scripture and faithfully living out the torturous, earthly assignment He'd been given. At the end of that excruciating time of trials, Jesus preached and gathered the men who would become His disciples. Matthew 4 ends this way:

> Jesus went throughout Galilee, teaching in their synagogues, proclaiming the good news of the kingdom, and healing every disease and sickness among the people. News about him spread all over Syria, and people brought to him all who were ill with various diseases, those suffering severe pain, the demon-possessed, those having seizures, and the paralyzed; and he healed them. Large crowds from Galilee, the Decapolis, Jerusalem, Judea and the region across the Jordan followed him. (Matthew 4:23–25)

Nothing is a surprise to our Heavenly Father. Immediately after Jesus was publicly claimed and esteemed by His father, He was led into the literal wilderness by the Holy Spirit. It was only after those forty days and nights that Jesus was launched into His public ministry. The intense time of persecution and physical stress on Jesus wasn't simply an incidental detour. It was all part of the plan, perhaps a refining fire.

You'll see the same principle in this book, in the stories of the mothers and daughters. Often their lives can seem wildly off track. Sometimes it's hard to understand the suffering that finds its way into their paths. Maybe that's true of your own journey. What's consistent throughout all of time is that God has purpose in each twist and turn, especially the ones we don't see coming. As Joseph told the very brothers who once plotted to kill him, and whom he later saved in their hour of need:

> You intended to harm me, but God intended it for good to accomplish what is now being done, the saving of many lives. (Genesis 50:20)

May you see the very same truth illustrated in the lives of the women on these pages, and in your own life too.

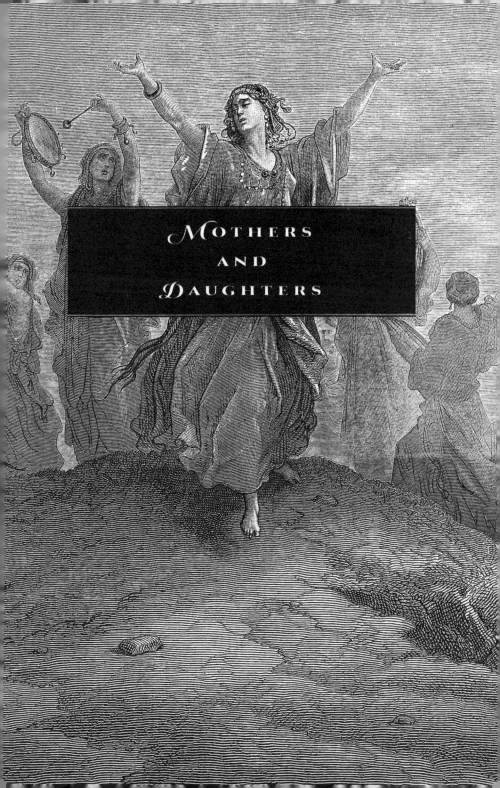

Mothers and Daughters

Mothers are our first protectors as we prepare to enter the world. Many of them pray over their children long before they have a name, storing up hopes and dreams for their little ones. The original connection and bond between mother and child is mysterious and unique—and lasts a lifetime. That's why it can be especially difficult when the path God charts for our children diverges from the one we may have mapped out in our own minds.

In this section we'll read about mothers who had great bravery and who suffered great loss. We'll also see the courage of daring daughters. Together we'll also witness the bonds that go beyond just earthly motherhood, seeing the beautiful connections that can encourage and inspire those we consider our spiritual mothers and daughters.

God gifted Jochebed, Miriam, Naomi, Ruth, Elizabeth, and Mary with the holy courage they needed to walk forward in His plans, even when they came as a surprise. These women found strength in their relationships and pointed one another to a deeper faith and trust in the designs our heavenly Father had for them. May we be inspired by their commitment, loyalty, and steadfast belief that God was working all things for His good through their lives.

JOCHEBED AND MIRIAM

(Genesis 37, Genesis 39–45:15,
Exodus 1–4:17, Exodus 15:20–21)

A DARK WORLD

The book of Genesis is full of mothers! From Eve to Sarah to Rebekah to Rachel and Leah, motherhood plays a key role in the early stories of the Bible. But we rarely see these mothers interacting with their children—and of the mothers who are named in Genesis, Leah is the only one whom the Bible mentions as having a daughter. Not until we get to Exodus do we meet the first mother/daughter pair we see interacting with each other in Scripture—Jochebed and Miriam. In a way, they are the only mother/daughter pair we include in these pages. The others we will journey along with in this book are related by marriage (Ruth and Naomi) or by cousinhood (Elizabeth and Mary).

When we venture into the extraordinary book of Exodus, we see the full power and beauty of the mother/daughter bond—just as the book of Exodus shows us the magnitude of God's relationship with His people, Israel. The wisdom of the Bible reveals both of these miracles for us together, and the story of God's intimate relationship with His people—not just Abraham and his family, or Jacob and his sons, but also the Israelite people as a whole—begins here, with the loving bond between mother and daughter at the beginning of an extraordinary story.

Genesis shows us how Jacob's twelve sons grew to become a distinct people with their own customs and identity. Exodus takes us the next step, showing us how the Israelites then entered into relationship with God, not as individuals, but as a group: as the newly formed people of God. Exodus is about the birth of Israel as a nation, and at the very start of this divine adventure we meet Jochebed and Miriam. It is through the bravery and sacrifice of this mother and daughter that the entire story of Scripture begins to unfold. What a gift God gives us in the biblical account marked by the faith, creativity, and courage of these two women!

But before we dive in, let's take a look back. Hundreds of years before Jochebed and Miriam arrived on the scene, the Israelites came to Egypt in a time of crisis. Their journey was enabled by a great man, a "chosen one" who had to go into exile and rise to power in a foreign land before he was finally in place to save Israel.

It all started with a serious case of sibling rivalry. Though Jacob had many sons, Joseph was the offspring of Jacob's beloved wife, Rachel. But there were eleven other sons, both from Jacob's other wife (and Rachel's sister), Leah, as well as sons born to Rachel's and Leah's servants—as was customary at the time. That Jacob favored Joseph over all his brothers was no secret; he even made his favorite son a special robe to wear. Here's how that overt favoritism went over with Joseph's older siblings:

> When his brothers saw that their father loved him more than any of them, they hated him and could not speak a kind word to him. (Genesis 37:4)

Joseph must have been fully aware of both his favored position and his brothers' jealousy over it. Yet, when he had dreams that seemed to signal an even further elevation of his status, he didn't hesitate to share them.

Joseph had a dream, and when he told it to his brothers, they hated him all the more. He said to them, "Listen to this dream I had: We were binding sheaves of grain out in the field when suddenly my sheaf rose and stood upright, while your sheaves gathered around mine and bowed down to it."

His brothers said to him, "Do you intend to reign over us? Will you actually rule us?" And they hated him all the more because of his dream and what he had said. Then he had another dream, and he told it to his brothers. "Listen," he said, "I had another dream, and this time the sun and moon and eleven stars were bowing down to me."

When he told his father as well as his brothers, his father rebuked him and said, "What is this dream you had? Will your mother and I and your brothers actually come and bow down to the ground before you?" His brothers were jealous of him, but his father kept the matter in mind. (Genesis 37:5–11)

Talk about not being able to read the room. Maybe Joseph spoke in humble confidence that the messages were not his, but divine in nature. In any case, his brothers were not enthused!

Things became so contentious that the brothers began to plot against Joseph, which was easy to do, since they were out in remote fields tending their herds. Barely restraining themselves from killing him, they instead trapped Joseph in an empty cistern when he came out to visit them. As the brothers ate their dinner, a group of traveling merchants headed to Egypt happened by. So, rather than murder Joseph, his brothers decided to sell him into slavery, and the travelers took him with them to Egypt. To round out their deception, the brothers slaughtered a goat and dipped Joseph's ornate robe in the blood, taking it back to their father. Jacob believed his beloved Joseph had been killed by a "ferocious animal" (Genesis 37:33) and fell into deep grief.

Did any of Jacob's sons who'd concocted this deceptive plan ever buckle under the guilt of what they'd done? Did they have regrets when they saw how heartbroken their father, Jacob, was? Whether they did—or didn't—wrestle with their treachery, Joseph's story was really just beginning. Once he reached Egypt, he was sold to Potiphar, one of Pharaoh's most esteemed officials. Joseph rose in prominence because of his trustworthiness and integrity.

> From the time he put him in charge of his household and of all that he owned, the LORD blessed the household of the Egyptian because of Joseph. The blessing of the LORD was on everything Potiphar had, both in the house and in the field. So Potiphar left everything he had in Joseph's care; with Joseph in charge, he did not concern himself with anything except the food he ate. (Genesis 39:5-6)

But there was trouble on the horizon. Potiphar's wife had noticed Joseph too, and she regularly tried to seduce him. Day after day, Joseph refused.

My master has withheld nothing from me except you, because you are his wife. How then could I do such a wicked
thing and sin against God?" (Genesis 39:9)

Yet Potiphar's wife continued her advances, and on a day when
they were all alone, she called to him again. Joseph refused again
and ran away from her so quickly that he left his cloak behind,
and Potiphar's wife took full advantage of that—framing him for
attempted rape. Despite what Potiphar knew about Joseph's character, he believed his wife's story and Joseph was thrown in jail.

It's easy to see how bitterness might have taken hold in Joseph's heart at this point. The most favored son in a flourishing
family, he seemed to be heading for greatness—then he faced a
series of advances and setbacks, and must have, in the moment,
felt like there was no plan or purpose after all. He was nearly
killed by his own brothers. Then his brothers sold him into slavery, but he was so honorable that he rose to the top of a prominent Egyptian household. We see no indication that Joseph had
dishonored the Lord or sinned, yet he was once again imprisoned and forgotten—but he was not forgotten by God. Despite
his circumstances, Joseph once again lived with virtue.

But while Joseph was there in the prison, the LORD was
with him; he showed him kindness and granted him favor
in the eyes of the prison warden. So the warden put Joseph
in charge of all those held in the prison, and he was made
responsible for all that was done there. (Genesis 39:20-22)

Thrown into one disastrous predicament after another, Joseph over and over again chose integrity and service to others.

That included the king's cupbearer and baker, who had angered their leader and wound up behind bars themselves.

This is where Joseph's ability to interpret dreams showed up again, a gift from God that would guide Joseph time and again. In prison, both the cupbearer and baker had vivid dreams, and as they searched for someone to interpret them, Joseph humbly said God could do that through him. Joseph's interpretations were good news for the cupbearer, that he would return to his position. But the baker's dream foretold his death. Joseph asked the cupbearer to remember him when he was released (as predicted), but the man did not . . . at least not for quite some time.

Years later, Pharaoh had two dramatic dreams of his own. As he searched for someone to explain them, that cupbearer remembered his debt to Joseph and told Pharaoh about his abilities. Joseph was quickly retrieved from the dungeon where he'd been imprisoned and called before Pharaoh.

"I cannot do it," Joseph replied to Pharaoh, "but God will give Pharaoh the answer he desires." (Genesis 41:16)

Pharaoh shared his peculiar dream, and led by God, Joseph predicted a cycle of seven years of abundance for Egypt followed by seven years of great famine. Joseph counseled Pharaoh to find a "discerning and wise man" to put in charge of Egypt's land and to manage the coming trouble (Genesis 41:33). Guess who, despite years of slavery and unjust captivity, was chosen to become only second to Pharaoh in all the land?

Then Pharaoh said to Joseph, "Since God has made all this known to you, there is no one so discerning and wise as

you. You shall be in charge of my palace, and all my people are to submit to your orders. Only with respect to the throne will I be greater than you." (Genesis 41:39–40)

Talk about redemption! Joseph's early dreams had put a target on his back, but his willingness to be God's messenger for the cupbearer, baker, and then Pharaoh changed everything—not only for him, but also for the nation of Israel to come.

It is easy to doubt God's plan and provision when we are struggling. I can only imagine how Joseph must have felt at times: despondent, wrongfully accused, and stripped of his most basic human rights. It must have felt doubly confusing after the prophecies of his childhood. I believe there is purpose in our pain, the twists and turns we didn't see coming in our journey, the things we would never willingly choose to face. In all of Joseph's story we never see him lashing out at God or denouncing his reliance on Him. If anything, we see him take every opportunity to turn potential earthly glory away from himself and directly to his heavenly Father.

The amazing story that unfolds from this point is one for the ages. As God guided Joseph to predict, Egypt had years of great bounty. Joseph oversaw the efforts to collect and save the surplus, which would sustain the people through the desperate years of crushing famine that followed. When that happened, people came from around the region seeking help—including Joseph's long-estranged brothers. In Genesis 42–45, you can read the astonishing story of Joseph's ability to provide for the very brothers who schemed to get rid of him forever. It had been so long since their cruelty to Joseph that they didn't even realize the man standing before them was their own flesh and blood.

When Joseph finally revealed his identity to his brothers, he didn't take a victory lap. I'm not gonna lie; I suspect I would have been lacing up my sneakers! *Just make them sweat for a bit. You DESERVE an apology!* Instead, we once again see the humble man of God Joseph had proven to be.

> And now, do not be distressed and do not be angry with yourselves for selling me here, because it was to save lives that God sent me ahead of you. For two years now there has been famine in the land, and for the next five years there will be no plowing and reaping. But God sent me ahead of you to preserve for you a remnant on earth and to save your lives by a great deliverance. So then, it was not you who sent me here, but God. He made me father to Pharaoh, lord of his entire household and ruler of all Egypt. (Genesis 45:5–8)

In other words, Joseph was saying, *Guys, I know you tried to make sure you'd never see me again. It's okay! God had this whole thing planned. It's not your fault.*

Not only was Joseph in a position to save his family, but he also had such enormous favor with Pharaoh that his entire family was able to move and settle into "the best part of the land" (Genesis 47:11). That's how the nation of Israel began her centuries of residence in Egypt, with Joseph celebrated and revered. The Israelites flourished for hundreds of years, but by the time of Jochebed and Miriam, this success was seen as a threat to the Egyptian leadership.

Then a new king, to whom Joseph meant nothing, came to power in Egypt. "Look," he said to his people, "the Israelites have become far too numerous for us. Come, we must deal shrewdly with them or they will become even more numerous and, if war breaks out, will join our enemies, fight against us and leave the country."

So they put slave masters over them to oppress them with forced labor, and they built Pithom and Rameses as store cities for Pharaoh. But the more they were oppressed, the more they multiplied and spread; so the Egyptians came to dread the Israelites and worked them ruthlessly. They made their lives bitter with harsh labor. (Exodus 1:8–14)

The integrity and humility of Joseph, which had saved the Egyptian people, was now nothing but a distant memory, and the reality for Jochebed and Miriam was one of brutal slavery and zero freedom. The people of Israel had gone from being honored guests in Egypt to resented foreigners to enslaved outsiders. But as we'll see, the story of Joseph and the story of Moses have more than a few parallels.

It's within this oppressive existence that we find the Israelites multiplying so quickly that Pharaoh hatched a murderous plan. He called in the Hebrew midwives and told them plainly: if a Hebrew woman gave birth to a girl, they could let the baby live; but they were to kill any male baby who came along. It's possible the midwives could have lied to the mothers, and in that world of high infant mortality an accidental newborn death would have been believable. Pharaoh's plan, for all its diabolical evil, was a sound one. But these women of valor decided not to go along.

> The midwives, however, feared God and did not do what the king of Egypt had told them to do; they let the boys live. (Exodus 1:17)

By the way, Pharaoh noticed that the Hebrews continued to have male babies—and that they were living. He demanded an explanation.

> The midwives answered Pharaoh, "Hebrew women are not like Egyptian women; they are vigorous and give birth before the midwives arrive." So God was kind to the midwives and the people increased and became even more numerous. (Exodus 1:19-20)

So Pharaoh moved on to plan B. He commanded that every male child born into a Hebrew family was to be thrown into the Nile River.

It is nearly too painful to picture the horror of a newborn baby being thrown into a river to drown—no exceptions, no hope. Imagine being a Hebrew mother, awaiting the day of her child's birth—knowing that a girl would live (though probably in lifelong servitude or slavery) and a boy would be killed. It was in this dark world that Jochebed became pregnant with Moses. I wonder what conversations she might have had with young Miriam about her pregnancy and the danger the growing baby could face. Even though she lived in a culture of oppression and poverty and fear, Jochebed had a family. There is something very hopeful about the fact that the Hebrew people continued to thrive despite near-constant persecution. We often see that when God's people are in the crucible of suffering they grow—in deeper commitment and often in number.

When Jochebed delivered Moses, Scripture makes clear he was special. We're told in Exodus 2:2 that Jochebed "saw that he was a fine child." Let's unpack two things here. First, the original word for *saw* indicates something more complex. Jochebed had a deeper perception—possibly a vision—about the child she had just given birth to. It was something more than just looking upon her precious child with adoration. As for the words *a fine child*, we see that concept repeated in the New Testament references to Moses: "At that time Moses was born, and he was no ordinary child" (Acts 7:20) and "they saw he was no ordinary child" (Hebrews 11:23).

A prophetic vision of the great destiny of a child happens again and again in the Bible. Joseph was special because he was the first child of the formerly barren Rachel. But Joseph was also given a prophetic glimpse into his future. It seems that this loving slave woman Jochebed was given similar divine insight about her baby boy, and it gave her courage. Not only did Jochebed recognize that her son was unique, but that awareness also gave her the strength to resist the command to take his life. Instead, she hid him for three months.

This mother was courageous *and* crafty. When she realized she could no longer conceal Moses, Jochebed coated a basket with tar and pitch, essentially making a baby ark for him. She made a plan and used the resources she had. Jochebed placed the basket among the reeds on the bank of the Nile River—the very place she'd been commanded to send her baby to die. She knew Moses had a special destiny, so to give him a chance at that life, Jochebed let her infant son go. The word for this basket is the same used to describe Noah's ark in Genesis 6. What a striking parallel! In both situations, water could destroy and take life, and in both stories we see God's provision for survival through these unique vessels. In both cases, human hands worked to craft God's means of escape—preserving His people for great plans ahead.

With Moses tucked into Jochebed's "ark" and placed along the banks of the Nile, her daughter—Moses's big sister—Miriam stood watch nearby, as the Lord provided a miracle.

> Then Pharaoh's daughter went down to the Nile to bathe, and her attendants were walking along the riverbank. She saw the basket among the reeds and sent her female slave to get it. She opened it and saw the baby. He was crying, and she felt sorry for him. "This is one of the Hebrew babies," she said. (Exodus 2:5-6)

Whatever the edict Pharaoh had laid down for the destruction of Hebrew sons, it appears his daughter's heart was filled with compassion instead. And Miriam was there to leverage that kindness!

> Then his sister asked Pharaoh's daughter, "Shall I go and get one of the Hebrew women to nurse the baby for you?"
>
> "Yes, go," she answered. So the girl went and got the baby's mother. Pharaoh's daughter said to her, "Take this baby and nurse him for me, and I will pay you." So the woman took the baby and nursed him. (Exodus 2:7-9)

In this scene, Miriam did two incredibly brave things. First, she stepped forward and addressed Pharaoh's daughter, a child putting herself squarely before one of the most powerful people in Egypt. She abandoned the safety of her hiding spot. She could have stayed put in a hidden place, and then, when the coast was clear, run back to her mother to tell her the good news. That would have been a happy ending. But Miriam didn't do that. Instead, she did a second brave thing: she spoke up and offered a solution that would either expose her family's secret or buy them more time with this vulnerable baby.

It is breathtaking to think about the risks Miriam took. She must have observed the princess long enough to be reasonably sure she would not ask probing questions about how that baby wound up there along the Nile, but it was still a risk. What if her mother was subjected to questioning about the baby? Or if Miriam herself was? Apparently, Miriam didn't stop to think about any of that. She saw a way to reunite her young brother with his devoted mother, keeping him safe and their family together. What a paradox that Pharaoh's plan was to subdue the Hebrew people by killing their sons, and it turns out a group of females thwarted his plan. Jochebed fought to save her son. Miriam boldly stepped up to protect him. Then Pharaoh's own daughter took pity on him and spared his life!

Can you imagine the weeping, the rejoicing, the laughter, maybe even dancing that must have happened in Moses's modest home that night? Could there have been anyplace in Egypt filled with more joy than the humble house of slaves whose child had just been restored to them? The faith and courage of this mother/daughter team put them in place to be ready for the miracle God delivered. Sometimes we, too, are called into action in a way that may seem strange to the world around us. If we are proceeding in God's will, then we can trust His guidance as modeled by Moses's parents. They were so confident in the favor of God on their son that "they were not afraid of the king's edict" (Hebrews 11:23). What a beautiful place we find ourselves in when we rest secure in the knowledge that God has the situation firmly in His hands.

Jochebed, having acted in obedience and faith, then had the blessing of raising her own son—rather than mourning his death. Per the custom of the time, it's likely she nursed and nurtured him for at least two to three years. Think of the wisdom and knowledge she poured into this young child, firmly rooting him in the ways and traditions and beliefs of the Hebrew people. All along, God was scripting Moses's story, equipping and preparing him to be uniquely qualified and positioned to save the entire nation of Israel. Jochebed's life is a perfect example of the impact and eternal importance of motherhood. The spiritual foundation she laid during her son's most formative years would make all the difference decades later, when Moses struggled with and then ultimately followed God's calling on his life. Jochebed also raised Miriam, who became a prophetess and leader among her people, and Aaron, who was the founder of Israel's priesthood. Their home must have been filled with deep reverence and commitment to the God of their fathers. Together, this trio of siblings would lead their people to freedom under God's direction and protection.

After Jochebed had the miraculous opportunity to raise her young son, she took him to Pharaoh's daughter. We don't know what Jochebed named her baby boy, but his adoptive mother gave him the name Moses, saying, "I drew him out of the water"

(Exodus 2:10). And because God is always doing the unexpected, this is not the story of a young prince raised as a slave, but of the slave raised as a young prince. God elevated the young boy born into slavery to a palace instead. When Jochebed lay in her bed at night dreaming of a happy ending for her beloved little baby, could she have envisioned something this phenomenal? Maybe she actually did! We know she saw something exceptional in her newborn son, enough to make her so bold as to disobey Pharaoh's order to kill him. Perhaps Jochebed's faith buoyed her with the assurance that God would protect and prepare this child for big things in the years to come.

Mothers across the ages have prayed over their children, asking God to protect and guide them. Few would dare to imagine that their three children would grow up to lead a nation, but that's exactly what happened to the family of Jochebed.

But it's also critical to remember that Moses, the man who led Israel out of slavery in Egypt, spent decades running from his ultimate destiny in a way that would break any mother's heart. The tragedy started when Moses tried to become his people's savior too early. We don't know much about his years growing up as part of Pharaoh's household, but we do know that he clearly identified with his Hebrew brothers and sisters when it came to their ongoing struggle. What's not apparent is how they viewed him. He'd been raised in a palace by the enemy. Did Moses have an overly confident view of his role as the potential "savior" of a people he may not have truly understood or fully identified with? In Exodus 2, we see him not only observing the harsh labor conditions the Hebrews were under but also witnessing something even more egregious—and committing a crime of his own.

He saw an Egyptian beating a Hebrew, one of his own people. Looking this way and that and seeing no one, he killed the Egyptian and hid him in the sand. The next day he went out and saw two Hebrews fighting. He asked the one in the wrong, "Why are you hitting your fellow Hebrew?"

The man said, "Who made you ruler and judge over us? Are you thinking of killing me as you killed the Egyptian?" Then Moses was afraid and thought, "What I did must have become known." (Exodus 2:11-14)

Moses's desire to save his people is understandable. After hundreds of years, Joseph's adventures must have become the stuff of legend to an enslaved people, the sort of story you tell around the campfire at night to wondering children. To Moses, a slave elevated to being a prince, it probably seemed like a reflection of his own life! Surely, it felt like God had placed him in the ideal position to save Israel from their harsh treatment. But God's plans were quite different. We can't know what was going through Moses's head when he killed the Egyptian, but it must have been a devastating blow to realize that not only were his people not falling in line—accepting him as a leader—but that his crime was the subject of gossip. He'd been betrayed by the people he saw as his own. In a moment, all his privilege—and his seeming golden future—was stripped away.

Like Joseph "the dreamer," Moses was about to be wrenched away from what seemed like a settled destiny. God was sending His chosen one into the wilderness, where he would be prepared for a role he didn't expect at all.

This must have been devastating for Jochebed. Like Mary weeping for Jesus, Moses's mother must have been devastated by her son's exile. Moses, Jochebed's son, the one she gazed upon after his birth with certainty about his favored destiny, was now a murderer who would soon be on the run. His sin was no secret, and Pharaoh was so furious we're told "he tried to kill Moses" (Exodus 2:15). Moses took off, armed with plenty of reasons to abandon Egypt for good. For decades following his decision to flee, he built a life in the wilderness, away from both the royal life he'd enjoyed and the plight of the oppressed Hebrew people.

Surely, Jochebed heard of what had happened with her son, that he was guilty of taking another's life. Did she wonder how this played into the plans God had for him? I imagine Jochebed prayed for her son all the years he was being educated and raised at the palace. It would only make sense she would continue to pray while he was on the run, far from home, building a completely different life from what she'd probably thought he would.

I know many women who began praying for their children long before they were even pregnant, asking God to draw them close to Him and to watch over them. When I was in college, I used to go on training flights with a friend who was building his hours as a pilot. It was a tiny plane, and the trips were short. I thought it was a fantastic opportunity, but I remember my mom saying to me, "Don't tell me when you're going; just let me know when you're back safe on the ground!" But I *wanted* my mom to know in advance. Why? Because she's a bona fide prayer warrior, and I knew she was always covering my adventures in prayer. How many mamas out there have burned the midnight oil, interceding for a child who's gone astray?

The prayer of a righteous person is powerful and effective.
(James 5:16)

And what a beautiful thing it is when all those prayers and the foundations mothers laid with those children ultimately bring them back home.

Start children off on the way they should go, and even when they are old they will not turn from it. (Proverbs 22:6)

That's exactly what happened with Moses, but not without him running in the opposite direction of the destiny Jochebed saw for him from the very earliest days of his life.

While Moses was sprinting from his past, his people—the ones he left behind—were desperate for a different future.

The Israelites groaned in their slavery and cried out, and their cry for help because of their slavery went up to God. (Exodus 2:23)

Exodus tells us that God heard their pleas and remembered the covenant He had made with Abraham, Isaac, and Jacob. And He was about to draft a very unwilling Moses to get the job of delivering the Israelites done. Before, Moses wanted to be a warrior savior, saving his people by the strength of his hand. But like Joseph, he had to go through a period of suffering—a "wilderness" period—when he had to rely on God and build a new life before he was offered the opportunity to be a liberator for his people. He must have thought he would be like Joseph at first: a kingly leader, perhaps second-in-command to Pharoah like Joseph was, but his privileged youth was a bit of narrative misdirection. It would be an elderly Moses, weather-beaten after years of labor as a shepherd, his youthful self-confidence shattered, who would take on the might of Egypt—with his words.

You've likely heard how the Lord got Moses's attention with a burning bush in the desert, something I believe would snap us all to attention. Look as God outlined His plan:

The LORD said, "I have indeed seen the misery of my people in Egypt. I have heard them crying out because of their slave drivers, and I am concerned about their suffering. So I have come down to rescue them from the hand of the Egyptians and to bring them up out of that land into a good and spacious land, a land flowing with milk and honey—the home of the Canaanites, Hittites, Amorites, Perizzites, Hivites and Jebusites. And now the cry of the Israelites has reached me, and I have seen the way the Egyptians are oppressing them. (Exodus 3:7-9)

Okay, Moses may have been thinking, *what exactly does this have to do with me?* At that moment Moses was already hiding his face in fear. Then the special favor his mother, Jochebed, had seen decades before, which made her so certain about him that she defied a king, began to unfold.

So now, go. I am sending you to Pharaoh to bring my people the Israelites out of Egypt. (Exodus 3:10)

Excuse me? Long after Moses fled in guilt and fear, God was asking him to return to the scene of the crime. Not only that, but he'd also be in charge of getting the entire Hebrew population out of Egypt.

> But Moses said to God, "Who am I that I should go to Pharaoh and bring the Israelites out of Egypt?" (Exodus 3:11)

This is where it gets good! Whenever God clearly directs us to take on a seemingly impossible task, we can rest in the knowledge that He's the one who's actually going to be getting the job done.

> And God said, "I will be with you. And this will be the sign to you that it is I who have sent you: When you have brought the people out of Egypt, you will worship God on this mountain." (Exodus 3:12)

Moses wasn't quite convinced.

> Moses said to God, "Suppose I go to the Israelites and say to them, 'The God of your fathers has sent me to you,' and they ask me, 'What is his name?' Then what shall I tell them?" (Exodus 3:13)

Moses still remembered being rejected by his people. He was still the same loner kid, only now he didn't even have the privileges of his Egyptian childhood to insulate him from being forsaken by the Hebrews. In my head, I hear this next part in a booming, thunderous voice from heaven.

God said to Moses, "I AM WHO I AM. This is what you are to say to the Israelites: 'I AM has sent me to you.'" (Exodus 3:14)

The Lord God Almighty was not messing around. That special child Jochebed held in her arms eighty years earlier was about to fulfill his destiny, whether he felt ready or not. God gave Moses specific directions about exactly what to say and to whom. He told him to assemble the elders of Israel and let them know God had been watching over them all during their misery—and that good things were coming. The Lord assured Moses the elders would listen, but that's not the only speaking assignment he'd have. Moses was directed to go directly to Egypt's king and demand the Israelites be allowed to leave. Even after God showed him the incredible signs and wonders Moses would be able to perform in order to convince any doubters, Moses remained a doubter himself!

Moses said to the LORD, "Pardon your servant, LORD. I have never been eloquent, neither in the past nor since you have spoken to your servant. I am slow of speech and tongue."

The LORD said to him, "Who gave human beings their mouths? Who makes them deaf or mute? Who gives them sight or makes them blind? Is it not I, the LORD? Now go; I will help you speak and will teach you what to say."

But Moses said, "Pardon your servant, LORD. Please send someone else." (Exodus 4:10–13)

It's easy, isn't it, to look at Moses in judgment. How in the world could you have come face-to-face with God, be shown miracles, have His full backing, and say: *No thank you?* But I know I've done it myself! God was not pleased, but He reminded Moses about his eloquent brother, Aaron. Yes, another one of the trio of champions Jochebed raised. God told Moses, "I will help both of you speak and will teach you what do to" (Exodus 3:15).

What follows in the next several chapters is a roller-coaster ride of tragedy and triumph. Together, the brothers confronted Pharaoh as God poured out His judgment on the Egyptians over and over again. When the Israelites finally burst forth from Egypt, in the wake of incredible miracles and with unmistakable divine intervention, there was enormous celebration as the Red Sea split wide open for the Israelites to walk on dry land. Those waters then swallowed up the entire Egyptian army that had been pursuing them. And that's when we see the other member of the sibling trio alongside her brothers once again.

> Then Miriam the prophet, Aaron's sister, took a timbrel in her hand, and all the women followed her, with timbrels and dancing. Miriam sang to them:
>
> > "Sing to the LORD,
> > for he is highly exalted.
> > Both horse and driver
> > he has hurled into the sea."
> > (Exodus 15:20–21)

The brave little girl had grown into a history-making prophetess and leader. The wise daughter we watched skillfully navigate her helpless infant brother to safety grew into a voice of God's prophecy and guidance for His people.

Again and again, we see that God highlights women and their roles in bringing about His bigger plans. Jochebed models faith for us. She was a woman so in tune with God that she was able to see an extraordinary vision for her son. That trust in God gave her the holy courage to defy an evil king's murderous order. She used what she had and released her precious baby to God's plan. It can be tough for us to surrender our loved ones to God, and Jochebed did it more than once.

I remember the excitement I felt going off to college as a seventeen-year-old freshman, so much so that I went the first two weeks without ever calling home. I think my mom was trying to give me space, but she finally broke down and called—letting me know in no uncertain terms that she expected her baby to check in on a more regular basis. I'd spent my senior year of high school itching to spread my wings, often clashing with my saint of a mother. But the truth was, I wasted many hours on campus at Liberty University fearing the worst. My parents were in Florida, twelve-plus hours away by car, and at least a connection or two via plane. Some nights I lay awake in bed wondering how quickly I could get home if something happened to them. It took up a lot of my mental space, but I finally realized it wasn't healthy. God never wants us to treasure His gifts to us more than Him, the Giver of those gifts. It's something I have to remind myself of regularly, and what better example than Jochebed?

What do we need to pack up in an ark and set free on the Nile? Is it social media, cultivating the perception of a perfect life? Maybe it's pursuing a relationship that's not meant to be, or chasing money and professional achievement. Maybe it's the security of your position in church or the awards your kids are winning. It can be the way you judge someone else or the harsh self-talk tearing you down from inside. None of us is immune. Personally, I often have to do reality checks on what—or who—I may be elevating above God Himself. So, let's commit to packing that stuff in a basket and launching it out. We can trust that the Lord will honor our sacrifice.

Heavenly Father, grant us the fortitude to love and trust You as Jochebed and Miriam did. Help us to fully devote ourselves to Your will, knowing You alone search the depths of our hearts and are fully aware of the infusion of courage we need in order to follow You. Grant that we may always hope for a way out of darkness when our own eyes see none, and may our love be a light and a place of refuge for all those in need.

Jochebed and Miriam Study Questions

1. What did Jochebed risk in order to save Moses, and why was she willing to do it? (Exodus 2:2; Acts 7:20; Hebrews 11:23) Do you believe God can give a mother insight beyond what human eyes see on the surface? How can that propel the way she prays for and directs her child?

2. What feelings do you think Jochebed experienced when it was time to send Moses to Pharaoh's daughter? Has God ever asked you to release someone—or something—you loved dearly to His greater plan? How do you reason through those kinds of decisions?

3. For years, Moses was on the run, away from his family and struggling with the role God had planned for him. Have you ever shied away from something God called you to do? What do we know about God's ability to equip us to accomplish when He's asking us to step out in faith? (Exodus 3, 4) Have you ever tried to talk God out of something? Did you eventually see how His plan was better than yours?

4. Have you ever watched as a child or loved one seemed to get way off track? How do you pray for or counsel them while you wait and hope they return?

5. Miriam, Aaron, and Moses were key leaders in Israel's escape from slavery. What does it say about Jochebed that she raised these three siblings who ultimately found their way back to each other to accomplish God's miracles? They were flawed, and prove that sibling rivalry was alive and well in biblical times. (Numbers 12) How does their story illustrate God's ability to work through flawed people?

RUTH AND NAOMI

(Book of Ruth)

NAOMI THE MOTHER

In *Women of the Bible Speak,* we considered Ruth's life in connection with the life of Tamar—another woman who knew what it was to be an outcast and a stranger, someone people despised and perhaps pitied. We saw beauty come from the mess that Tamar made when God redeemed her mistakes and wove her story into the lineage of Jesus Christ. In this book, we're going to view Ruth through the lens of being a daughter and the relationship she built with the woman who became her second mother, Naomi. Their journey together began in shared grief, but resulted in deep joy and deliverance. It started in earnest when Ruth took a true leap of faith, a bold step that led her away from her family of birth but into the promises of God and a new family.

Again and again in Scripture, we see examples of "found families." Adoption is a theme God beautifully illustrates for us repeatedly in the Bible, leading up to the adoption of Christians as sons and daughters of God.

But when the set time had fully come, God sent his Son, born of a woman, born under the law, to redeem those under the law, that we might receive adoption to sonship. (Galatians 4:4–5)

The language is woven throughout the New Testament. In Romans 8:15, Paul encouraged new believers by reminding them that "the Spirit you received brought about your adoption to sonship."

And, of course, Jesus's own story is one of adoption. He was known as the son of Joseph, but Joseph was His adoptive father—a man who took on a divine assignment that upended his life and called him to a challenging journey. Scripture indicates that Joseph was a good father to Jesus, keeping Him (along with His younger half-brothers and half-sisters) safe in Nazareth, watching over his family, and likely teaching Jesus everything he knew about the carpentry and building trades. All of the themes of adoption that run throughout the New Testament have roots in the "found family" stories of the Old Testament.

One of the most beautiful examples we get of a "chosen family" bond in the Old Testament is the relationship between Ruth and her mother-in-law, Naomi. The book of Ruth starts with the story of Naomi, one of heartbreaking loss.

In the days when the judges ruled, there was a famine in the land. So a man from Bethlehem in Judah, together with his wife and two sons, went to live for a while in the country of Moab. The man's name was Elimelek, his wife's name was Naomi, and the names of his two sons were Mahlon and Kilion. They were Ephrathites from Bethlehem, Judah. And they went to Moab and lived there. (Ruth 1:1–2)

Like countless families before and after them, Naomi and Elimelek had fled their home country, Judah, during a time of famine, searching for a better life for themselves and their sons. They appeared to find it in the nearby land of Moab, after what was about a fifty-mile journey. So, this family was away from the customs and traditions of their own people, living in a new land as outsiders, when tragedy struck.

Now Elimelek, Naomi's husband, died, and she was left with her two sons. They married Moabite women, one named Orpah and the other Ruth. After they had lived there about ten years, both Mahlon and Kilion also died, and Naomi was left without her two sons and her husband. (Ruth 1:3–5)

Naomi, in a foreign land with two sons, lost her husband. The grief of becoming a widow in those times was exacerbated by the devastation of losing the family's financial provider. Though nearly all of Naomi's stability was shattered when her husband died, she had two sons. Both of them had married Moabite women, creating a new family unit and the possibility of precious grandchildren on the way. Naomi's grief over the loss of her husband had its consolation, because she had her sons—until she didn't. Both Mahlon and Kilion died.

Overnight, Naomi's situation became dire. Three men had been in the place of making sure she would be safe and secure, but not one was left. Naomi was bereft. With no husband or sons, she faced poverty and death in Moab. But then a glimmer of hope: Naomi received word that the situation at home had improved, providing the possibility of returning to her own land.

When Naomi heard in Moab that the LORD had come to the aid of his people by providing food for them, she and her daughters-in-law prepared to return home from there. With her two daughters-in-law she left the place where she had been living and set out on the road that would take them back to the land of Judah. Then Naomi said to her two daughters-in-law, "Go back, each of you, to your mother's home. May the LORD show you kindness, as you have shown kindness to your dead husbands and to me. May the LORD grant that each of you will find rest in the home of another husband." (Ruth 1:6–9)

We see something of Naomi's faith here, because she heard "that the LORD had come to the aid of his people by providing food for them" (Ruth 1:6). Notice that Naomi attributed Judah's recovery from famine to God's action. At the heart of her story, although Naomi was grieving, she could see God's hand in her own life and in the lives of her people. So she stepped out in faith: she packed up to take her weary, grief-stricken heart back home to her people.

As much as Naomi, Orpah, and Ruth needed one another, Naomi selflessly stopped to think of her daughters-in-law and the life they could still have—complete with family, children, and the security of a new marriage. This trio of women had suffered so much together, and that must have bonded them deeply. It's understandable, then, that the two young women didn't want to abandon Naomi to fend for herself. The best hope that Ruth and Orpah had for a prosperous life—for any life at all, really—was to stay in Moab, where they could find new husbands among their own people. What possible chance did these two Moabite women have of finding husbands in a country where they would be strangers and immigrants? For Orpah and Ruth to pledge to stay with Naomi was an act of extraordinary love.

The actions of her daughters-in-law hint at what kind of person Naomi must have been, generous of spirit and loving, leading the three of them through devastating sorrow and loss. For both her daughters-in-law to desire to remain with her in their widowhood instead of returning to their own families suggests Naomi must have been a remarkable individual. Orpah and Ruth were willing to risk their own futures, and leave behind their own country and their own families, just to stay with her!

Too often our society feeds us the poisonous narrative of the critical, unpleasant mother-in-law—the jealous or overbearing mother-in-law, the nosy mother-in-law, the hostile mother-in-law. But that does not reflect the experience of many women. For many of us, the mother we adopt in marriage becomes a cherished part of our lives, and in many cases she becomes as important to us as our own mothers. I certainly won the mother-in-law lottery myself. Jouetta Bream and I have the most important things in common: faith in Christ and an unwavering love for her son, Sheldon. But we couldn't be more different as individuals! She can whip up a feast for thirty people in an afternoon without glancing at a single cookbook, and I can . . . well, boil water. She raised six kids and made it look easy. I struggle to keep our lab, Biscuit, on track!

I remember early in our marriage when I was a young attorney, feeling overwhelmed and working around the clock. As we chatted on the phone she'd occasionally ask what I was making for dinner. I felt attacked because everyone knows Sheldon didn't marry me for my cooking, but I soon realized she was just trying to make conversation with her new daughter-in-law, not point out my lack of domestic talents. We bonded over what we did share in common: a love for Jesus, Hallmark movies, books, sweets, *her* cooking, and that amazing son of hers.

What joy it must have been for Naomi, mother of two boys, when they welcomed two daughters into the family. The Hebrew word for daughter-in-law is *kallah,* and it's a complicated word. It's sometimes translated as "bride," and it is used in that sense in the romantic imagery of the Song of Songs. But the root of the word *kallah* is *kalal,* which means "perfected" or "made complete." A daughter-in-law is not just a bride for the son, but she adds to the entire family unit. Naomi's daughters-in-law were her family, and for her to leave them behind in Moab would be to leave a part of her heart there as well.

In the touching and beautiful scene of Naomi's departure, we can see the family bond these three women had forged in their shared grief and mutual affection. Because she loved her daughters-in-law, Naomi was unwilling to let them sacrifice themselves in this way. She urged them to "go back" (Ruth 1:8), and she underlined the command by telling them to return to their homes—the homes of their birth mothers, not of the mother they had adopted. *Start your lives over,* she was telling them. *Go home and get remarried. Coming with me makes no sense.*

But Orpah and Ruth refused to listen.

Then she kissed them goodbye and they wept aloud and said to her, "We will go back with you to your people." But Naomi said, "Return home, my daughters. Why would you come with me? Am I going to have any more sons, who could become your husbands? Return home, my

daughters; I am too old to have another husband. Even if I thought there was still hope for me—even if I had a husband tonight and then gave birth to sons—would you wait until they grew up? Would you remain unmarried for them? No, my daughters. It is more bitter for me than for you, because the LORD's hand has turned against me!" (Ruth 1:9–13)

Naomi was clear: there was nothing for Orpah and Ruth down the road she was about to travel. There is some wordplay involved in verse 13, because Naomi's name means "sweet" or "pleasant." It is the opposite of "bitter" (*marah*), and she was being frank with them that only bitterness awaited her in her homeland.

We see Naomi's generosity here too. Naomi had a long, hard, and dangerous journey ahead of her, and it would have made sense to take the young women along for companionship and safety. Certainly Naomi would have been less lonely, less afraid, if they accompanied her. The perils for a woman traveling alone during that time are hard for us to imagine. For most of us, unpleasant travel means a bored toddler or long TSA checkpoint line. Naomi would have been risking something altogether different. The trip would have been a challenge even with a man along to protect her, but a solo woman would have been exposed in totally different ways. Yet Naomi did not request, or even accept, Orpah's and Ruth's help. Instead, she made the selfless choice of pushing them away. And Naomi's orders were obeyed . . . almost.

At this they wept aloud again. Then Orpah kissed her mother-in-law goodbye, but Ruth clung to her. "Look," said Naomi, "your sister-in-law is going back to her people and her gods. Go back with her." But Ruth replied, "Don't urge me to leave you or to turn back from you. Where you go I will go, and where you stay I will stay. Your people will be my people and your God my God. Where you die I will die, and there I will be buried. May the LORD deal with me, be it ever so severely, if even death separates you and me." When Naomi realized that Ruth was determined to go with her, she stopped urging her. (Ruth 1:14–18)

Even though Naomi urged her to turn back, Ruth refused. Many people look at this passage as an example of beautiful earthly love, and they are right. But what about looking at the passage in another way—as a model for evangelism? Naomi was the first person in this story to talk about the Lord, and that became a consistent theme in Naomi and Ruth's relationship. She reminded Ruth that going back home would mean going back to "her people and her gods" (Ruth 1:15), but Ruth was persistent. She wanted to go with Naomi, and she wanted to worship Naomi's God. In the ancient Near East, religion was very closely linked to nationality and a people's culture. Ruth was consciously leaving all that behind and clearly choosing to align with the God of Naomi and her people.

So often when we think about evangelism, we assume we need to prepare a three-point presentation, quoting Bible verses and complex points of theology to convince someone to accept Christ. But evangelism isn't always about a polished presentation or theological defense. Sometimes, it's just about being with another person—spending time with him or her, building a relationship, living out our faith in front of that person, and talking about God in the natural conversations that arise. It's easy to see how that could have been what happened as Naomi and Ruth walked through some valleys together, both literally and figuratively!

The Bible doesn't tell us exactly why Ruth chose to leave her gods for the God of Israel, but apparently there was something about Naomi that caused Ruth to want to follow her God—perhaps it was the way Naomi trusted God even in difficult times, or maybe Ruth watched Naomi worshiping the Lord and realized that there was something very unique about her God. Whatever the reason, we know that Ruth's relationship with Naomi was strong, and it drew her to want to follow the Lord. What if we adopted this as our model of evangelism—living out our walk with the Lord in such a way that our lives are constantly communicating His hope and truth? It was her devotion to Naomi that led Ruth to make one of the greatest declarations of love in the Bible: "Your people will be my people, and your God my God" (Ruth 1:16).

And this was more than just adoption; it was Ruth choosing to leave her own people and land. She then became a child of Israel, bringing her Moabite heritage into the family of God. It was a heritage her great-grandson David would later remember, for when he went on the run from Saul's armies, he sent his family to shelter in Moab (1 Samuel 22:3-4). Ruth's conversion is a beautiful example of how God intended Israel to influence the world—as He said in His promise to Abraham, "All peoples on earth will be blessed through you" (Genesis 12:3)—and an early example of the sort of evangelism Christ would command His church to carry out. From this point on, Naomi and Ruth were no longer just mother-in-law and daughter-in-law; they became mother and daughter. Ruth had declared that Naomi's people were hers, which meant that Naomi was now her mother, in every sense of the word.

When the two women made their way back to Bethlehem, Ruth asked permission from Naomi to glean in the field of Boaz, Naomi's wealthy relative. Gleaning was hard work, the process of going behind those who had reaped the crops in order to pick up anything beneficial they'd left behind.

> **Now Naomi had a relative on her husband's side, a man of standing from the clan of Elimelek, whose name was Boaz. And Ruth the Moabite said to Naomi, "Let me go to the fields and pick up the leftover grain behind anyone in whose eyes I find favor." Naomi said to her, "Go ahead, my daughter." (Ruth 2:1-2)**

We can see both Ruth's deference to the authority of Naomi and also Naomi's blessing of her decision with the phrase "my daughter." These two were doing life together as a family unit, as incredibly challenging as it was.

RUTH THE DAUGHTER

At this point in the story, the focus moves to Naomi as a mother and her plan for the women's survival. Ruth was obedient— faithful in her willingness to fulfill what Naomi had in mind. But before we look at that plan, we should look a little bit more at the relationship of these women with God.

In the first chapter of the story, Naomi mentioned the name of God five times. She blessed her daughters-in-law in the name of the Lord, telling them, "May the LORD show you kindness, as you have shown kindness to your dead husbands and to me" (Ruth 2:8). She then prayed that the Lord would grant them future prosperity and new husbands (Ruth 2:9). Finally, when her daughters-in-law resisted leaving her, she told them that staying with her would be a losing proposition for them, because "the LORD's hand has turned against me" (Ruth 2:13). It can be hard for us to track in English, because we are used to thinking of the terms *God* and *Lord* as interchangeable in Scripture, but in Hebrew they are very different terms.

When we see the name *Lord* in the Old Testament—most often in small capital letters as LORD—we are seeing not a translation of the original Hebrew word but a substitution for it. The word that lies behind "LORD" is the Hebrew word best rendered in English as YHWH, and sometimes we see English approximations of that as "Yahweh" or even "Jehovah." The word *God* is not specific to the people of Israel; after all, all the nations around them had gods, in the sense of a generic word. Egypt had gods, Canaan had gods, Moab had gods; every place had its own unique god or gods. But the name YHWH is the personal name of Israel's God—a name so holy, so revered, and so specific that even to speak it aloud came to be seen over the centuries as a sign of disrespect. This practice is still followed by devout Jews of all sorts today, and the personal name of God is translated as "Adonai" (meaning "my lord") or just as "Lord," as in most Christian translations.

Why is this important? Because Ruth used the very specific name of God—the name of Naomi's God, of Israel's God—when she told Naomi that she would not leave her. Ruth had already told her that Naomi's God would be her God, using the generic name for any deity. But then she said, "May the LORD deal with me, be it ever so severely, if even death separates you and me"

(Ruth 1:17). The word that she used there—LORD—is the word YHWH. She invoked the very name of God, as only a devout Jew would do, and in doing so, Ruth made it clear that she was joining herself not just to Naomi but also to the people of Israel, as a devoted daughter of both Naomi and the God of Israel. All of this is important because it places God at the center of the relationship between Ruth and Naomi. Their love for each other was deepened by the faith they came to share. It was not biology that united this mother and daughter pair but their faith in Yahweh, the Lord God—the God of her ancestors, in the case of Naomi, and the faith of her mother, in the case of Ruth.

So faith was at the center of this mother-daughter relationship, and the strength and power of adoption (of a new faith and a new family) is at the core of their story. With that faith, these two women—alone and powerless, without any means of support—were strengthened and protected. As believers we are grafted together and into a spiritual family, a place where we are immediately and forever bonded to those who share our faith. There must have been times when Naomi wondered whether her daughters-in-law would embrace her faith or continue on with the gods they'd been raised to worship. As she stood there on the road back to Judah, she might have thought, *Ah well, it's too late now.* But that was exactly the moment when God moved in and captured Ruth's heart. The moment that is just beyond despair is often the moment when God acts—in Ruth's and Naomi's lives, in the lives of Jesus's disciples, and in our own lives too.

So what happened when Ruth and Naomi—bonded first by marriage and then by faith—committed to each other and their trust in God? Well, for one thing, they attracted the notice of a kind, generous man who shared their faith, and also happened to be a relative:

> Just then Boaz arrived from Bethlehem and greeted the harvesters, "The LORD be with you!"
>
> "The LORD bless you!" they answered.
>
> Boaz asked the overseer of his harvesters, "Who does that young woman belong to?" The overseer replied, "She is the Moabite who came back from Moab with Naomi. She said, 'Please let me glean and gather among the sheaves behind the harvesters.' She came into the field and has remained here from morning till now, except for a short rest in the shelter." So Boaz said to Ruth, "My daughter, listen to me. Don't go and glean in another field and don't go away from here. Stay here with the women who work for me. Watch the field where the men are harvesting, and follow along after the women. I have told the men not to lay a hand on you. And whenever you are thirsty, go and get a drink from the water jars the men have filled." (Ruth 2:4–9)

The very first thing we hear Boaz say is the name of God. He greeted the men working for him with a blessing, showing us that he was a man who carried God with him into his daily life and work. Watch too the way that Boaz honored Ruth in the way he first addressed her. The men in the fields might have dismissed her as just "the Moabite" (Ruth 4:6), but Boaz knew better. He knew that Ruth was a daughter of Israel, and his own relation through Naomi. As a man of faith, Boaz fulfilled the command of Scripture to care for the stranger by extending generous hospitality to her.

Ruth may have been both surprised and curious about why Boaz was so kind and protective of her.

At this, she bowed down with her face to the ground. She asked him, "Why have I found such favor in your eyes that you notice me—a foreigner" (Ruth 2:10)?

Boaz didn't see her question as an opportunity to brag about what a godly person he was. Instead, he shone the spotlight on Ruth, and the humble, devout daughter of Israel *she* was.

> Boaz replied, "I've been told all about what you have done for your mother-in-law since the death of your husband—how you left your father and mother and your homeland and came to live with a people you did not know before. May the LORD repay you for what you have done. May you be richly rewarded by the LORD, the God of Israel, under whose wings you have come to take refuge." (Ruth 2:11-12)

The wording of that last phrase uses the Hebrew word *kenaphaim,* which you can find all throughout the Old Testament. It paints the picture of the way a bird gathers her babies close to her for protection, just as God does with His children. Ruth was in that same position, and she expressed her deep gratitude for the kindness of Boaz for his part in that umbrella of grace. He then gave her even more.

> "May I continue to find favor in your eyes, my lord," she said. "You have put me at ease by speaking kindly to your

servant—though I do not have the standing of one of your servants."

At mealtime Boaz said to her, "Come over here. Have some bread and dip it in the wine vinegar."

When she sat down with the harvesters, he offered her some roasted grain. She ate all she wanted and had some left over. As she got up to glean, Boaz gave orders to his men, "Let her gather among the sheaves and don't reprimand her. Even pull out some stalks for her from the bundles and leave them for her to pick up, and don't rebuke her." (Ruth 2:13–16)

When Ruth returned home that night, she told Naomi about this man's extraordinary kindness to her—the way he had provided food for her (which she shared with Naomi) and made sure that Ruth had an abundance of leftover grain to glean. When Naomi asked the man's name, she was overjoyed to learn that it was Boaz. In fact, Naomi called him *our* close relative" (Ruth 2:20), once again making sure that Ruth (and the reader) understood that Ruth was now family. Once again the name of God was invoked by Naomi in blessing:

"The Lord bless him!" Naomi said to her daughter-in-law. "He has not stopped showing his kindness to the living and the dead." She added, "That man is our close relative; he is one of our guardian-redeemers." (Ruth 2:20)

The phrase translated here as "guardian-redeemer" is an odd one. You'll sometimes see the phrase "kinsman-redeemer" used as well. We don't have any equivalent in English, but the idea is that the nearest relative had a responsibility to assist a family member in trouble, primarily in the context of redeeming or buying something back for someone in need. These were prosperous, financially stable men with standing in their community. Often the word is simply translated as "redeemer" in English. Of course, Naomi and Ruth lived in a time when, if the poor had no one to help them, they starved—which frequently happened. In order to prevent that, Jewish law (Leviticus 25:25-55) set up a system of accountability, so that families would be obligated to help their own—even distant relations.

Scripture talks a lot about the role of a "redeemer," and God Himself is often identified in the Old Testament as "Redeemer"—rescuer of the people of Israel. The Psalms refer to God as "my Rock and my Redeemer" (Psalm 19:45), and Job at the end of all his trials said, "I know that my redeemer lives, and that in the end he will stand on the earth" (Job 19:25). But when we talk about a "redeemer" in terms of the law—the kind of legal redeemer Boaz was—the context is one of obligation and responsibility. Boaz was *expected* to do right by these women if there wasn't another closer relative able to step up. He took that kindness far beyond duty, making Ruth feel accepted and welcomed.

We can see the same devotion in the way Ruth protected and served Naomi. As a widow herself, Ruth was under no obligation to abandon her own life in Moab to provide for her mother-in-law. In fact, the expectation of her Moabite society was just the opposite. Naomi was a foreigner heading back to her home and away from all of Ruth's roots. When Ruth acted to "redeem" her mother-in-law from poverty and abandonment, she was acting only out of love. And Naomi's commitment to Ruth returned the affection. When Naomi learned what Ruth had gleaned in Boaz's field, she urged her not to wander off elsewhere: "It will be good for you, my daughter, to go with the women who work for him, because in someone else's field you might be harmed" (Ruth 2:22). The two women were dedicated to each other, bound together by shared sorrows and joys—not any legal duty. Their communities dictated no framework or expectations obligating them to one another.

Scripture is always pointing us to the ultimate Redeemer, who ransomed us not out of obligation but out of unconditional love.

For the grace of God has appeared that offers salvation to all people. It teaches us to say "No" to ungodliness and worldly passions, and to live self-controlled, upright and godly lives in this present age, while we wait for the blessed hope—the appearing of the glory of our great God and Savior, Jesus Christ, *who gave himself for us to redeem us* from all wickedness and to purify for himself a people that are his very own, eager to do what is good. (Titus 2:11-14)

What a glorious display of love. Christ, perfect and unblemished by sin, came to earth and suffered enormous pain to win back every single one of us. He didn't wait until we were worthy; He knew we never could be!

But God demonstrates his own love for us in this: While we were still sinners, Christ died for us. (Romans 5:8)

The poverty and despair that Jesus redeems us from is our own debt of sin. His rescue plan for us has nothing to do with money. He gave Himself. God acted as our Redeemer, solely motivated by His love for us. No law or court told Him to pay the price for us. Ruth's choice to actively embrace Naomi and her people solely out of love is a perfect Old Testament foreshadowing of the extravagant sacrifice Christ would display on the cross centuries later.

MOTHER AND DAUGHTER TOGETHER: BETTER THAN SEVEN SONS

So how did their story, one that began with such heartbreak and loss, ultimately play out? Naomi and Ruth, mother and daughter by choice, wound up with blessings beyond what they could have imagined. Naomi's maternal instincts on behalf of Ruth were strong. Remember Naomi's impassioned plea that the young widow go rebuild her life? Ruth's bold choice to follow Naomi and join her people led them somewhere altogether different. And in those new circumstances Naomi saw a way forward for Ruth, the selfless daughter-in-law who had abandoned her own hopes in order to protect her.

> One day Ruth's mother-in-law, Naomi, said to her, "My daughter, I must find a home for you, where you will be well provided for. Now Boaz, with whose women you have worked, is a relative of ours. Tonight he will be winnowing barley on the threshing floor. Wash, put on perfume, and get dressed in your best clothes. Then go down to the threshing floor, but don't let him know you are there until he has finished eating and drinking. When he lies down, note the place where he is lying. Then go and uncover his feet and lie down. He will tell you what to do."

"I will do whatever you say," Ruth answered. So she went down to the threshing floor and did everything her mother-in-law told her to do. (Ruth 3:1–6)

To the modern reader Naomi's idea can read as ... strange. Or worse, it can seem overtly sexual, which it was not. Naomi was not urging Ruth into a compromising situation. Uncovering a man's feet and crouching at them was a way for a woman to place herself under his protection—a sort of act of submission. It was saying, *Here I am. It's up to you whether you're willing to assume this role.* But Naomi's plan showed humility and discretion, because the entire plan hinged on its secrecy. Imagine this scene if it had taken place in front of the gates of the city, where all public business was conducted. Boaz may have felt guilted or coerced into committing to Ruth. She and Naomi didn't want to put him in that position; instead, they quietly and privately reached out to the man who had already shown them so much generosity.

Boaz would have a choice to make, and that's a constant theme running through this little book of just four chapters. Isn't it amazing how much is packed into these few pages? So many of the themes of Scripture are here: the presence of faith, the power of adoptive love, and the importance of free choice. Ruth and Naomi chose each other and pledged to meet their enormous challenges together. Boaz had a choice too. If he accepted the idea of being Ruth's protector in marriage, then he would do so free of any public pressure. He could have sent Ruth away, and no one would ever have known it had happened. Discretion was an act of generosity from Naomi and Ruth. They invited Boaz to decide freely whether he would take on such a serious obligation, and he did! Happily, of course, Boaz gladly accepted Ruth's offer.

We see mother and daughter conferring afterward, and Ruth accepting Naomi's wise counsel of patience:

> When Ruth came to her mother-in-law, Naomi asked, "How did it go, my daughter?" Then she told her everything Boaz had done for her and added, "He gave me these six measures of barley, saying, 'Don't go back to your mother-in-law empty-handed.'" Then Naomi said, "Wait, my daughter, until you find out what happens. For the man will not rest until the matter is settled today." (Ruth 3:16–18)

It is such a human moment: the daughter excitedly relating everything that has happened, and the mother saying, *Wait now, slow down; let's not get ahead of ourselves.* In this short exchange, we can really see their relative ages and how completely they have become mother and daughter.

Naomi of course was right: Boaz did settle the matter immediately. He took their private agreement of the threshing floor into the public space of the city gate. There he publicly proclaimed himself the protector of Naomi and Ruth by announcing that he would buy Naomi's husband's ancestral property from her. Here we see a little bit of Boaz the clever businessman too. Naomi had another kinsman, a relative closer than Boaz, and Boaz very generously offered this man the opportunity to buy the property. At first, the closer relative was eager to do so. *But wait,* Boaz said, *there's a catch.*

> Then Boaz said, "On the day you buy the land from Naomi, you also acquire Ruth the Moabite, the dead man's widow,

in order to maintain the name of the dead with his property." At this, the guardian-redeemer said, "Then I cannot
redeem it because I might endanger my own estate. You
redeem it yourself. I cannot do it." (Ruth 4:5-6)

The full package, Boaz explained, was that along with the land
came the lovely Ruth the Moabitess. That meant the purchaser of
the land would also have to marry Ruth and allow his firstborn
son by her to be counted the heir of her dead husband, so the
line of Naomi's husband Elimelek would continue in Judah. I can
picture the man's face as it all began to sink in. *Ohhhhhh*. He
hastily bowed out and let Boaz assume the responsibility.

It is interesting to note the reason the man says he "cannot
do it" (Ruth 4:6): because he might "endanger his own estate"—
meaning that if his children by Ruth were counted as the grand-
sons of Elimelek, then they would inherit both his land and
Elimelek's. The relative's own estate might get swallowed up in
Elimelek's, and he did not want that to happen. Preserving the
family name and lineage was paramount in those times, something men would have been highly motivated to do. And while
we don't know that man's name, we do know the names of all
of Boaz and Ruth's descendants, including the most important
one: Jesus Himself. Even if in the short term Ruth's children were
named for Elimelek, it was Boaz's righteousness and generosity—
and Ruth's courageous conversion and loyalty—that left the legacy we still remember today.

The story ends as it began, with Naomi and Ruth.

So Boaz took Ruth and she became his wife. When he
made love to her, the LORD enabled her to conceive, and

she gave birth to a son. The women said to Naomi: "Praise be to the LORD, who this day has not left you without a guardian-redeemer. May he become famous throughout Israel! He will renew your life and sustain you in your old age. For your daughter-in-law, who loves you and who is better to you than seven sons, has given him birth." Then Naomi took the child in her arms and cared for him. The women living there said, "Naomi has a son!" And they named him Obed. He was the father of Jesse, the father of David. (Ruth 4:13–17)

Is it possible to read the end of the book of Ruth and not feel tears of joy? It's truly a love story, though not solely in the conventional sense. It's the love of a young woman whose heart was devoted to her mother-in-law, and whose mother-in-law cherished her as a true daughter. They tied their survival to each other and to God, watching as His provision unfolded in the most unlikely way. I've always loved that, in a society that prized sons in so many ways, the women of Bethlehem celebrated Ruth's worth as more than that of seven sons! The foreigner, the woman, the convert, the adopted one: all the things that made Ruth an outsider wound up being the characteristics that made her extraordinary. One day, that little hamlet would become famous for being the birthplace of her great-grandson, called the city of David.

There are two things that we should note about this beautiful ending to the story of Ruth and Naomi. The first is the presence of *faith*, Naomi's from the beginning and then Ruth's by deliberate choice. It anchored their relationship and kept their eyes firmly on the God of Israel, the truest Redeemer. The gift of a son for Ruth was rightly ascribed as a gift from the Lord, and these blessings had their origin in God.

The second thing to note is Naomi's relationship to her precious grandson, Obed. When the Bible tells us that Naomi "took the child in her arms and cared for him" (Ruth 4:16), that doesn't mean just that she did all the things a loving grandmother would do. Obed was the continuation of the line of Elimelek, something Naomi had probably feared was lost forever. Naomi had lost her husband and her two sons, but this newborn son provided what she may have given up on long ago: a family legacy and fresh hope. Ruth and Naomi's bond united them so profoundly, so powerfully, and so completely that the joys of one became the joys of the other.

Love changes things, but the biggest thing it transforms is *us*. Ruth and Naomi were sustained through life's darkest hours by their devotion to each other. They were different people, from distinct places and backgrounds, but their love united them on a fundamental level. "Naomi has a son!" proclaimed the women of Bethlehem in joy. But we know God provided that miracle—which would echo through the generations—by first providing Naomi a treasured gift when she needed it most: a daughter.

Lord God, our Guardian, Protector, and Redeemer, we thank You for the gift of motherhood and daughterhood. We praise You for the mothers and daughters in our lives. May we notice all the ways You are always working to bring the miracle of love into our stories. Help us to love selflessly like Ruth and guide lovingly like Naomi.

Remind us that our mothers and our daughters are not always related to us by blood and that together we can support each other through all of life's challenges. May our love bring us the same unity of spirit and faith that Ruth and Naomi shared, and grant us the gift one day of rejoicing with them in Your heavenly kingdom.

Ruth and Naomi Study Questions

1. What does the Bible tell us about the beauty of adoption both in Ruth and Naomi's story and in the New Testament language about Christian believers' adoption into the family of God? (Galatians 4:4–5; Romans 8:15)

2. How much of a sacrifice and commitment was Ruth making to Naomi in the well-known words she spoke in Ruth 1:16–18? Why do you think these words are so often used in marriage ceremonies today? How did Ruth's actions also demonstrate her devotion?

3. Ruth modeled great humility. How does God honor that in her story, and how can He use it in our lives? (Ruth 2:11–12; 3:3–4:17)

4. What sacrifice did Boaz make in taking Ruth to be his wife and in the birth of their son, Obed? Where is Obed in the lineage of Christ?

5. What can we learn from the commitment Ruth and Naomi made to each other and how we as Christian women can develop spiritual motherhood and daughterhood in our lives? Is there someone in your life you could develop this kind of relationship with?

ELIZABETH AND MARY

(Malachi 4, Luke 1:5–80)

Of all the mothers and daughters we meet in this book, Elizabeth and Mary are unique in a number of ways. Both of them had miraculous paths to motherhood, and both gave birth to men who changed the world forever. Like Jochebed and Miriam, this pair stood at the crossroads of salvation history. Like Naomi and Ruth, they were mother and daughter spiritually, not biologically. But there is a crucial difference in the relationship between Elizabeth and Mary—and it's not just that one of these women was the mother of Jesus. It's that both were mothers in their own right. Elizabeth was the biological mother to John the Baptist and a spiritual mother to Mary, and Mary was mother to Jesus. They model for us the very specific way God can place spiritual encouragers in our lives when we need them most, whether we are linked by blood or by heaven.

Mary and Elizabeth were cousins rather than mother and daughter, though Elizabeth was much older than Mary. God in His wisdom linked them beyond just their familial ties. Each would experience something wondrous, at nearly the same time. They were able to comfort and reassure in ways only those two women could possibly understand in that season of their lives. God prepared divine journeys for each of them, and He provided their companionship to each other to fortify them through what must have been complicated times.

WHO IS ELIZABETH?

Luke is the only Gospel that tells us the story of Elizabeth and her husband, Zechariah. From the opening chapters of his letter, Luke made clear that he took relating the events surrounding Christ's life with great responsibility. He wrote in verse 3, "I myself have carefully investigated everything from the beginning." Luke went on to tell the reader he compiled this account "so that you may know the certainty of the things you have been taught" (Luke 1:4). Luke authored not only the longest Gospel, but he's also believed to be the author of Acts. That means he recorded a sizeable portion of the New Testament, filled with key details and important specifics for us to read today.

Luke offers us the only account of the birth of John the Baptist, who served as the forerunner of Christ and whose arrival was also touched by divine intervention. He begins by introducing us to John's parents, Zechariah and Elizabeth, as "upright in the sight of God, observing all the Lord's commandments and regulations blamelessly" (Luke 1:6). They were both from priestly lineages, with Zechariah serving as one of thousands of priests in that day. It's also fascinating to note that when their story starts, God has been silent for roughly four hundred years. When the Old Testament ends in Malachi 4, the Lord says:

> I will send the prophet Elijah to you before that great and dreadful day of the LORD comes. He will turn the hearts of the parents to their children, and the hearts of the children to their parents. (Malachi 4:5–6)

And then Israel heard nothing directly from the Lord for centuries. Against this backdrop, Zechariah was faithfully serving as a priest, and he was doing so while he and Elizabeth ached for lack of a child. She was barren, and when we meet them the Bible says they "were both well along in years" (Luke 1:7).

In those days most of society viewed the lack of a child as God's punishment or withholding of favor, but Luke made it clear that both Zechariah and Elizabeth were "upright in the sight of God" and living out His commands without flaw. As we see in the biblical stories of Sarah and Hannah and others, God often has a plan beyond our understanding when infertility is part of our story. Just as in the lives of those Old Testament mothers, God was weaving His purposes into Elizabeth's story too. As the Israelites had been waiting to hear from the Lord for centuries, Zechariah and Elizabeth too had waited decades to hear from Him in the midst of their own circumstances.

Luke tells us that Zechariah had reported for his priestly duties; the lot fell to him to go into the temple for the offering of incense. Priests served two one-week periods each year, and there were thousands of them. A priest could easily go a lifetime without ever being chosen to carry out this special task. Nothing is ever a surprise to God, and you better believe Zechariah's selection to enter the temple was no mistake. That's where he encountered the stunning presence of an angel.

When Zechariah saw him, he was startled and was gripped with fear. But the angel said to him: "Do not be afraid, Zechariah; your prayer has been heard. Your wife Elizabeth will bear you a son, and you are to call him John. He will be a joy and delight to you, and many will rejoice because of his birth, for he will be great in the sight of the LORD. He is never to take wine or other fermented drink, and he will be filled with the Holy Spirit even before he is born. He will bring back many of the people of Israel to the LORD their God. And he will go on before the LORD, in the spirit and power of Elijah, to turn the hearts of the parents to their children and the disobedient to the wisdom of the righteous—to make ready a people prepared for the LORD."

Zechariah asked the angel, "How can I be sure of this? I am an old man and my wife is well along in years."

The angel said to him, "I am Gabriel. I stand in the presence of God, and I have been sent to speak to you and to tell you this good news. And now you will be silent and not able to speak until the day this happens, because you did not believe my words, which will come true at their appointed time." (Luke 1:12–20)

There is a lot to unpack here! First of all, no one had heard directly from God for four hundred long years, and now Zechariah was face-to-face with the angel Gabriel bringing him nearly unbelievable news. Second, remember where things left off in Malachi? Gabriel was echoing those long-ago promises back to Zechariah, telling him *he* would be the father of the one who would work "in the spirit and power of Elijah, to turn the hearts of the fathers to their children . . . to make ready a people prepared for the LORD" (Luke 1:17). Third, as most humans would, Zechariah had doubts and Gabriel was not amused. He rendered Zechariah mute until the birth of John, as Gabriel had prophesied. Bottom line, Elizabeth was going to be a mother!

The people waiting and praying outside the temple had become curious about what was taking so long. Imagine their confusion when Zechariah finally exited and tried to relate to them what had happened. I love that while he was finally able to communicate to them that he'd seen an angel, Zechariah stuck around to complete his time of service as a priest (Luke 1:23). Elizabeth probably knew none of this before Zechariah returned home. It had been quite a whirlwind: having his lot drawn to present the offering of incense, meeting an angel, finding out his wife would become pregnant and bear a son who would make way for the Lord, and being struck mute! Oh to be a fly on the wall for that "conversation" once Zechariah made it home. What a round of charades this must have been. *Honey, I saw an angel, and he told me you're going to get pregnant—yes, now—and give birth to the man who will introduce our Lord.* Did Elizabeth scream for joy? Was she afraid? Disbelieving?

There wasn't much time to debate because the very next verse tells us that Elizabeth became pregnant. Finally, motherhood—probably decades after she'd given up any hope! As a young couple faithfully following the Lord, they must have wondered and been heartbroken when month after month, year after year, their hopes of having a child grew dimmer and dimmer. But God was working through those delays and pain, scripting the perfect story to bring John the Baptist into the world to set the stage for Christ Himself.

Gabriel told Zechariah "your prayer has been heard" (Luke 1:13). How long had it been since Zechariah had prayed for a son? Was there a point when he assumed it was no longer even worth asking? Are there hopes and dreams you've abandoned, things you prayed over for years and then put on a shelf for good? We often cannot see how God is weaving together the threads of our lives until long after the tapestry is complete. He may present you with an answer you never imagined decades after your original request. I sometimes struggle mightily to bring about what I see as the perfect path forward, only to realize, when that season is in my rearview mirror, that the agenda I so desperately wanted to achieve was wildly inferior to God's design. I also believe some of what wounds us most on this earth won't make sense until we are in heaven, with an eternity to praise God for His infinite wisdom during the times we just couldn't see past our own pain.

Zechariah's name translates to "the Lord has remembered." How beautiful is that? Elizabeth means "my God is an oath," a marker and reminder of his faithfulness. Upon learning she was pregnant, Elizabeth directed all glory to God. "The Lord has done this for me," she said, noting that God had shown her favor (Luke 1:25). Because of Luke's detailed description of Elizabeth, we know she was clearly a godly and mature woman. Who better to serve as an encouragement, companion, and spiritual mother to Mary when her own miraculous news arrived? Several months into Elizabeth's pregnancy with John, the angel Gabriel paid a visit to Mary.

In the sixth month of Elizabeth's pregnancy, God sent the angel Gabriel to Nazareth, a town in Galilee, to a virgin pledged to be married to a man named Joseph, a descendant of David. The virgin's name was Mary. The angel went to her and said, "Greetings, you who are highly favored! The LORD is with you." Mary was greatly troubled at his words and wondered what kind of greeting this might be. But the angel said to her, "Do not be afraid, Mary; you have found favor with God. You will conceive and give birth to a son, and you are to call him Jesus. He will be great and will be called the Son of the Most High. The LORD God will give him the throne of his father David, and he will reign over Jacob's descendants forever; his kingdom will never end."

"How will this be," Mary asked the angel, "since I am a virgin?" (Luke 1:26–34)

In both Zechariah's and Mary's stories, Gabriel showed up and told them something truly incredible. Zechariah was devout but he responded with understandable fear and doubt. Scholars say Mary's response was more in line with curiosity. *I believe you; I just don't know how this will actually come about.* How incredulous would you or I be if an angel showed up and started prophesying about miraculous, supernatural events in our lives that would change the entire course of human history? It seems fitting that Gabriel told both Zechariah and Mary, "Do not be afraid" (Luke 1:13, 30). I sure would be—not only at the sight of an angel, but also at the news he was delivering. I find it rather impressive that neither of them fainted!

No one had heard from God in hundreds of years! It is a credit to the deep faith of both Zechariah and Mary that when an angel appeared before them, they didn't question it. They accepted the angelic presence with the confidence of faith, though they did have questions. There is a practical edge to both of them—a belief, but also a desire to know the nuts and bolts of how something so amazing would unfold—literally.

Gabriel answered Mary's question with not only an explanation but even more good news:

The angel answered, "The Holy Spirit will come on you, and the power of the Most High will overshadow you. So the holy one to be born will be called the Son of God. Even Elizabeth your relative is going to have a child in her old age, and she who was said to be unable to conceive is in her sixth month. For no word from God will ever fail." (Luke 1:35–37)

Gabriel immediately pointed Mary to "Elizabeth your relative" (Luke 1:36), who had been barren, and he urged her to consider that Elizabeth's pregnancy as a sign that nothing was impossible with God. Luke tells us Mary "hurried" to see Elizabeth (Luke 1:39). Mary must have been nearly overwhelmed with joy. She knew the pain Elizabeth had suffered, longing for a child it seemed she would never have. Mary also had some pretty spectacular news of her own. The two women were bound in miraculous motherhood, and Mary knew Elizabeth would welcome her news too. At a time when Mary must have wondered how she was going to share the news of her pregnancy with a flabbergasted community, she would never have to fear Elizabeth's reaction or doubt her support. That was clear from the moment Mary arrived.

When Elizabeth heard Mary's greeting, the baby leaped in her womb, and Elizabeth was filled with the Holy Spirit. In a loud voice she exclaimed: "Blessed are you among women, and blessed is the child you will bear! But why am I so favored, that the mother of my LORD should come to me? As soon as the sound of your greeting reached my ears, the baby in my womb leaped for joy. Blessed is she who has believed that the LORD would fulfill his promises to her!" (Luke 1:39–45)

Note how the Bible describes Elizabeth: "filled with the Holy Spirit" (Luke 1:41). Gabriel had already told Zechariah that their baby, John, would be Spirit-filled from birth (Luke 1:16). But when Mary and Elizabeth saw each other, we're told Elizabeth herself was filled with the Holy Spirit—and she began to prophesy. Before Mary could even explain her heavenly encounter, Elizabeth was speaking the truth of the divine pregnancy Mary was carrying. What a spectacular blessing for these mothers-to-be. These two women knew of each other's pregnancy before they each had a chance to share the news themselves. Elizabeth was blessed with a pregnancy long after she thought she could know the joy of having a child, and Mary was surprised by a pregnancy much earlier than she may have felt prepared for. Her spiritual mother, Elizabeth, would be there to share in the joys and challenges certain to come.

Elizabeth was a comfort and a guide to Mary, and she shows us generations later how to be a mentor or encourager. Our earthly relationships can never serve as a substitute for our fellowship with our heavenly Father, but they can be a deep source of consolation and wisdom. I'll never forget the time I called my dear friend Mariam in tears. I was in the midst of an ongoing season of living in chronic pain and had hit a new low. Life felt hopeless and meaningless as I stumbled through one day and into another. I prayed endlessly for relief and healing, but there came a time when I felt desperate for the guidance I knew Mariam possessed. I needed someone who represented God's compassion to me in flesh-and-blood form. I knew she couldn't physically heal me, but I've always viewed Mariam as a spiritual mother of sorts—someone tested by time and devoutly committed to humbly and joyously living out God's plans. I wept in the gazebo in her yard as she reminded me of God's promises and purpose in all our pain. She prayed over me that day, and I have no doubt she continues to include me in her requests before the Lord. Like Elizabeth for Mary, Mariam has always represented a source of acceptance and hope to me. While not a replacement for our personal connection to God, as women we can share reminders of His grace and mercy in our kindness to each other.

Beyond simple encouragement, Elizabeth's words to Mary were a confirmation of Gabriel's declaration, an expression of her own humility and praise for Mary's faith. It is important to keep in mind that because Elizabeth was filled with the Holy Spirit here, this was an act of prophecy on her part. She had no prior knowledge that Mary was pregnant, and no way of knowing. Elizabeth's proclamation had to give Mary added comfort, knowing that someone she already trusted and loved fully accepted the divine nature of her pregnancy. God knew well in advance that young Mary would be encouraged by mature Elizabeth's embrace of her situation, without question or doubt.

In her humility, Elizabeth asked, "Why am I so favored, that the mother of my Lord should come to me?" (Luke 1:43). The first person in Scripture to call Jesus "Lord" was Elizabeth. She declared the One who was coming, and that her own son would be the one to lay the groundwork for Him. Both Elizabeth and John would play roles in recognizing and proclaiming the divinity of Mary's baby, long before others also saw His true identity and mission. Pay attention also to the last thing Elizabeth said to Mary—which is also the last thing she says in the Bible. She announced to Mary, "Blessed is she who has believed that the LORD would fulfill his promises to her" (Luke 1:45).

Mary came to Elizabeth in a rush, as Scripture tells us. She was probably bursting with all sorts of confusing feelings: joy, wonder, fear, uncertainty. What would this mean for her future with her betrothed, Joseph? What would people say about her? And it wasn't just that. Mary literally could have been stoned to death over this out-of-wedlock pregnancy. I'm sure she wondered more than once why this had happened to her, of all people? She must have been wondering what was so special about her that God would choose her, a young girl from an insignificant Roman province, to bear the promised Messiah.

Elizabeth put her finger on exactly what it was that made Mary exceptional: "Blessed is she who has believed" (Luke 1:45). It wasn't Mary's purity of heart, her charity, her kindness, her modesty, or her wisdom that made her so favored by God—though she probably had all those qualities! Elizabeth went straight to the heart of the matter: Mary had believed. It was Mary's extraordinary faith that had set her apart. Elizabeth was speaking with direct inspiration from the Holy Spirit when she highlighted and praised Mary's trust in God's promises and plan. Mary committed to God—even when she couldn't understand exactly how He would bring the mysterious prophecy to pass. She still moved forward.

> "I am the LORD's servant," Mary answered. "May your word to me be fulfilled." (Luke 1:38)

Elizabeth saw and celebrated Mary's belief.

What follows is one of the most famous passages in all of

Scripture: Mary's Song of Praise, called the Magnificat (the Latin word for *magnifies*). It is a beautiful and remarkable poem that draws on the traditions of Jewish Scripture, from the prayer of Hannah through the promises of Isaiah. So often when we read Mary's song in church, or in a Bible study, we look solely at this one passage and fail to see its larger context. Everything that comes pouring out of Mary in these verses—all the poetry and fiery faith that have lit the heart of Christians for two thousand years—happened because of what Elizabeth told her. Elizabeth's perception gave Mary her *aha!* moment. Elizabeth's words enabled Mary's glorious proclamation. Elizabeth's Spirit-filled wisdom spilled over into Mary's soul and sparked her song.

When we read these words, perhaps we picture Mary as she declares them. But this time, try something a little different: imagine yourself as Elizabeth in this situation. Envision standing there and hearing Mary pour forth this inspired song of praise. Can you capture the experience of the pride and affection Elizabeth must have felt for her young cousin? Think of how proud it makes us when we see our own children, godchildren, nieces, or nephews making their first confessions of faith, when we realize that the seeds of faith have taken root in their hearts. Elizabeth must have felt the same indescribable joy, tenderness, and pride when she heard Mary's words.

> And Mary said:
> "My soul glorifies the LORD
> and my spirit rejoices in God my Savior,
> for he has been mindful
> of the humble state of his servant.
> From now on all generations will call me blessed,

for the Mighty One has done great things for me—
holy is his name.
His mercy extends to those who fear him,
from generation to generation.
He has performed mighty deeds with his arm;
he has scattered those who are proud in their inmost
thoughts.
He has brought down rulers from their thrones
but has lifted up the humble.
He has filled the hungry with good things
but has sent the rich away empty.
He has helped his servant Israel,
remembering to be merciful
to Abraham and his descendants forever,
just as he promised our ancestors." (Luke 1:46–55)

When Mary said that "the Mighty One has done great things for me" (Luke 1:49), she was echoing the words of Elizabeth when she said "the LORD has done this for me" (Luke 1:25). Mary mirrored Elizabeth's words of praise and gratefulness, giving God all the glory. What happens at the end of Mary's Song is often omitted, or just plain overlooked, but it tells us quite a bit about the significance of their relationship. When Mary had finished her song of praise, Scripture says, "Mary stayed with Elizabeth for about three months and then returned home" (Luke 1:56).

Let's consider the timeline here. After the angel Gabriel had left Mary, she "hurried" to share her news with Elizabeth, to rejoice in Elizabeth's good fortune, and to get her older cousin's help in digesting the astonishing developments. We know that Mary was relatively young, because the average age of betrothal at that time in Israel could have been anywhere between thirteen and eighteen years of age. Why didn't Mary run to her own mother with the news? Was it in part because God had graciously provided her with the knowledge that Elizabeth too was experiencing a miracle and would be in the best possible position to understand Mary's jumble of emotions? Why did Mary travel (apparently alone) into the hill country of Judea? This would not have been an easy, short stroll. To undertake it must have meant that Mary's affinity for Elizabeth and the help she would find in her home was worth the effort to get there. Both the immediacy of her visit and the length of her stay give us important information about how close Mary was to Elizabeth.

Mary likely felt a deep sense of security with Elizabeth in those early months. The two of them shared extraordinary secrets. Mary's pregnancy could have turned her into an outcast, a young woman viewed as impure and sinful by those who would not understand or believe her explanation. Once he knew, Joseph could have easily broken his commitment to her. She could have paid for the perceived fornication with her life. But the months in the safety of Elizabeth's home undoubtedly bolstered her faith and calmed her worries.

For three months, these women were living together daily—sharing their excitement and their dreams for the future and their babies, who would change the world together. Did they recount what Gabriel had said to Zechariah and then to Mary? Did they try to extrapolate just how Gabriel's prophecies would play out for the babies then resting in their wombs? Was Mary learning from Elizabeth about how her pregnancy would progress, what to expect? It would have been the most natural thing for an inexperienced, pregnant young woman to stay with her cousin and spiritual mother so she could learn firsthand about all the things that were going to be happening in her own body.

Was Mary also learning about what to expect for the birthing process? We know that when it came time for Mary to deliver, it appears she had no support system other than Joseph and some barn animals! Any lessons Mary had learned from Elizabeth were likely invaluable to Mary that night. So just as Elizabeth gave Mary spiritual strength, she also gave her practical wisdom. And that is exactly what a true spiritual mother does for her spiritual daughter: she sustains and supports her in spirit and in body.

When we think about the many different ways that women appear in the Bible, and the diverse roles they fill, we can see that the Bible offers us an incredibly rich portrait of all the things it means to be a woman. Rarely, however, do we see two women speaking to each other, and even more rarely about God. We see Rachel and Leah conversing, and we see Ruth and Naomi express their devotion to each other and lay plans for their future. Here, we see two women talking about their faith in God, encouraging each other as they experience His miracles, and expressing their gratefulness both to Him and to each other. We can glean new insights by reading through this pre-Christmas story and focusing on this supportive relationship, which may have gotten lost in the shuffle in the past. I don't know about you, but I unearth new treasures every time I dive into a passage I may have read hundreds of times. We should always approach Scripture this way: as though it were a precious jewel that we were holding to the light, mesmerized by its beauty, turning and rotating it in the hope that we will see some new and wondrous facet that we had never appreciated before.

The story of Mary and Elizabeth is like that, with so much

truth and beauty in one story, one devoted relationship. We see the way God moves in our lives, despite our own fears and uncertainties. We observe the way God's power and strength are revealed in the weak and seemingly insignificant of the world. In Mary's song of praise, we witness the sweep of salvation history and the supernatural power of the God who lifts up the humble and brings down rulers from their thrones—the God who is the Lord of history, as well as the Lord of our lives.

Ancient and medieval Christians were fascinated by this moment between Mary and Elizabeth, which they called "the Visitation of the Blessed Virgin Mary" or simply "The Visitation." It can refer to both Mary's arrival to see Elizabeth and the Holy Spirit's arrival within Elizabeth. One of the oldest images depicted in Christian places of worship or Christian homes was of this scene, the embrace of the two women. Sometimes the images even picture the babies inside them, so that the bodies of Mary and Elizabeth serve as a kind of frame for the young John the Baptist and Jesus, who also tentatively reach toward each other. The love of spiritual mother and daughter not only framed but also provided the actual human embodiment for the arrival of the gift of salvation for all humanity.

We don't know the circumstances of how Mary was brought up, or by whom, but from what little the Bible tells us we can see that Elizabeth was probably a significant part of that. The devout faith of Elizabeth informed the godly trust of Mary, "she who believed," and Mary's obedience made all of our lives as Christians possible. As brothers and sisters of Jesus, we too are spiritual children of Mary and spiritual grandchildren of the righteous Elizabeth, who gave thanks for the miracle the Lord had worked in her life.

We have no idea what happened to Elizabeth or when she died—and for that matter, we don't know those things about Mary either. We can guess that Zechariah and Elizabeth, who were older when John was born, probably died long before his work as John the Baptist began. So sometime before Jesus and John began their public ministries, Elizabeth had most likely died. Mary's husband, Joseph, was most likely dead as well, since Mary was traveling with Jesus at least at some points (John 2:1-12; 19:25; Matthew 12:47), and we see no mention of Joseph after Jesus's visit to the temple when he was missing around age twelve. This meant that as Jesus was starting to teach and preach, Mary had lost people very dear to her. In Elizabeth's absence, Mary was most certainly missing her mentor and spiritual mother as she watched her son—the one they had dreamed about together—be tortured and put to death.

This too is part of the bittersweet love between mother and daughter. As spiritual mothers, we pass on our wisdom to our spiritual daughters, knowing that we might not be able to be there for them when they need it the most. We might be absent from the darkest hours of their grief, many years down the road. As spiritual daughters, we love our spiritual mothers, knowing that there will come a time when they travel beyond our care and we will have to take the lessons of their strength and move forward, trusting that we will see them again in heaven. We can cherish the wisdom and strength they've poured into us, learning to become "she who has believed"—a light to the generations to come, as we were in turn enlightened by our own spiritual mothers.

Spiritual motherhood involves guiding and leading someone in faith. Not all of us will be called to biological motherhood, but we can all exercise the role of spiritual motherhood. We can lead young women to Jesus by word and example, becoming a sounding board for their questions and our challenges. For many Christians, this role is filled by a godmother or a trusted older woman in our faith community. Most of us can think of women who have served as role models to us and who have gently guided us along our faith journey. Sometimes those women are in our family, as Elizabeth was in Mary's family, and sometimes they are not, but they are always crucial to our spiritual growth. If they're still in our lives, let's be sure to thank them!

Our spiritual mothers also share in our joys and sorrows, and—most importantly—help us understand those unexpected twists and turns in light of our faith. In an effort to find the deeper meaning tucked into the events of our lives, they can guide us as we dig in and try to see how God is working. That's especially helpful when sorrow, pain, or confusion enter our journey. And when we are filled with joy, they are there to share in it—just as Elizabeth and Mary did all those centuries ago.

Lord God, grant us the strength to become spiritual mothers to those in need of our wisdom, strength, and love. Help us to mother those whose own mothers are gone or far away. Give us words of gentleness and encouragement for those daughters You place in our paths. Help us also to be thankful for the spiritual mothers You have blessed us with, who have nurtured faith in us and taught us how to be mothers in turn. May all our spiritual motherhood and daughterhood reflect Your love, deepening our trust in You and creating a dwelling place for Your Holy Spirit.

Elizabeth and Mary Study Questions

1. What do we know about the kind of woman Elizabeth was? Do you think she had given up on motherhood as part of her story? How does her story highlight the purpose in the period of waiting God sometimes asks us to walk through in order to fulfill His greater plans? (Luke 1:12–20)

2. Why do you think Gabriel told Mary about Elizabeth's pregnancy? (Luke 1:36–37)

3. How were Elizabeth and Mary perfectly equipped to encourage each other through extraordinary times? How can we point each other to deeper faith in God in the face of our own fears and questions?

4. Has someone in your life recognized and encouraged your faith walk as Elizabeth did for Mary? (Luke 1:45) What did that mean for you? Have you done that for someone else?

5. Have you seen the fruit of the seeds a spiritual mother planted in your life? What about in someone you invested in? How can we find spiritual mothers and daughters around us, and what's the eternal impact of investing in those relationships?

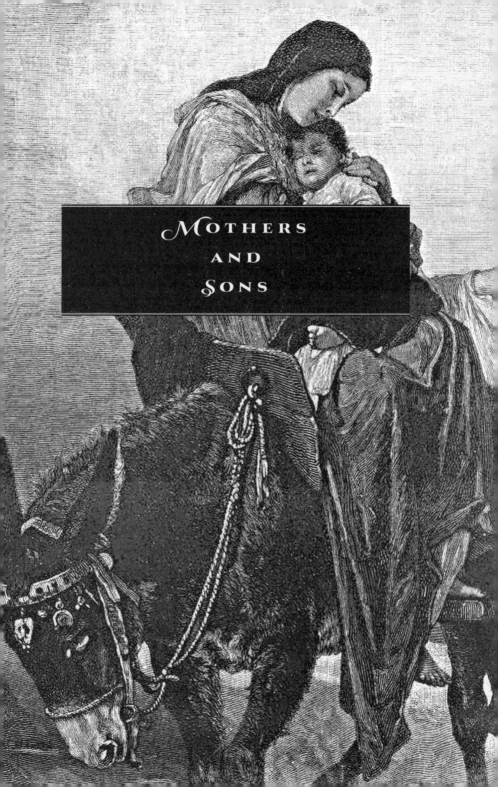

MOTHERS

AND

SONS

Mothers have enormous influence over their sons, for better or for worse. In the Bible we see examples of both. The positive serve as inspiration and encouragement for mothers seeking to propel their sons toward God's perfect design for their lives. The negative are a clear warning that attempting to scheme and deceive in order to help a child skip ahead will only serve to delay God's plans and bring great pain and dishonor in the process.

What do we communicate to God when we are willing to sin, lie, and undercut others in order to better position our children? How can we expect that the selfish aims we use as the foundation for our own desires will bring glory to God and His kingdom? We see the devastation an overly ambitious mother can cause when she's led astray by greed and disbelief.

But the Bible also provides us beautiful examples of brave, humble, righteous mothers willing to surrender their own hopes and dreams in favor of what God had planned. They model sacrifice, obedience and the ability to trust that God has the long-term good of their children in mind, even when they can't see it. It's not a path of pure, uninterrupted joy, but it is the way of ultimate peace and serenity.

REBEKAH

(Genesis 25:19–27:46, Genesis 33)

REBEKAH THE DAUGHTER

Have you ever known someone whose life seemed charmed: a perfect combination of natural gifts and golden opportunities? It seems like they've been set up for success and given a head start. It can be disheartening, then, to watch as they squander it all—either painfully unaware of their good fortune or possibly consumed by it. To see someone like this choose her own destruction can be puzzling at best and infuriating at worst. How could someone with every apparent advantage allow herself to become consumed by jealousy, insecurity, ego, or ambition?

God allows these kinds of stories to bubble up all through the Bible, so that we can learn from them. In journeying along with Rebekah, we see a life that started with incredible promise but veered into dangerous territory. Where were the off-ramps, the places where Rebekah could have corrected course? They were there, and by studying her it's my hope that we'll see those opportunities for redemption in our stories.

Rebekah was sought after, a bride chosen directly by God for Abraham's beloved son Isaac. As Abraham was nearing the end of his life, he began to focus on Isaac and the promises God had made regarding the favor and lineage that would flow through him. Abraham feared God and served Him faithfully. He had seen miracles and believed fully in the covenant God had made with him, promising that his descendants through Isaac would become a great nation and be blessed by God (Genesis 12:1–3). Abraham was living in a land apart from his people, but one that God had promised to give him and the generations that would follow through Isaac. For those reasons, Abraham had very specific instructions for the man he sent to find Isaac a wife from his own tribe. The man was Abraham's most trusted servant, the one he'd put in charge of his entire household.

> I want you to swear by the LORD, the God of heaven and the God of earth, that you will not get a wife for my son from the daughters of the Canaanites, among whom I am living, but will go to my country and my own relatives and get a wife for my son Isaac. (Genesis 24:3–4)

These were clear directives, but Abraham's representative had a critical question before he embarked on the long journey.

> The servant asked him, "What if the woman is unwilling to come back with me to this land? Shall I then take your son back to the country you came from?"
>
> "Make sure that you do not take my son back there," Abraham said. "The LORD, the God of heaven, who brought me out of my father's household and my native land and who spoke to me and promised me on oath, saying, 'To your offspring I will give this land'–he will send his angel before you so that you can get a wife for my son from

there. If the woman is unwilling to come back with you, then you will be released from this oath of mine. Only do not take my son back there." (Genesis 24:5-8)

Abraham was blunt: Isaac would need a wife willing to journey to a foreign land and help him build the legacy God had promised would be fulfilled in that place. So Abraham's servant swore an oath to him, gathered ten camels and all kinds of gifts, and set off.

The trip likely took weeks, and as the group approached the town of Nahor, where Abraham's brother lived, the caravan stopped. It just so happened to be the time of day when women from the town were out collecting water at the well. Abraham's steadfast servant called for some divine help.

Then he prayed, "LORD, God of my master Abraham, make me successful today, and show kindness to my master Abraham. See, I am standing beside this spring, and the daughters of the townspeople are coming out to draw water. May it be that when I say to a young woman, 'Please let down your jar that I may have a drink,' and she says, 'Drink, and I'll water your camels too'—let her be the one you have chosen for your servant Isaac. By this I will know that you have shown kindness to my master."

Before he had finished praying, Rebekah came out with her jar on her shoulder. (Genesis 24:12-15)

We're immediately told some things about Rebekah in the verses that follow. She was from the right family for Isaac, she was beautiful, and she was industrious.

The servant hurried to meet her and said, "Please give me a little water from your jar."

"Drink, my lord," she said, and quickly lowered the jar to her hands and gave him a drink.

After she had given him a drink, she said, "I'll draw water for your camels too, until they have had enough to drink." So she quickly emptied her jar into the trough, ran back to the well to draw more water, and drew enough for all his camels. Without saying a word, the man watched her closely to learn whether or not the LORD had made his journey successful. (Genesis 24:17–21)

Bingo! Was this the one? Abraham's servant kept a close eye on this woman, who seemed heaven-sent. She was certainly hospitable and hardworking. I've read that these camels could have consumed up to forty gallons of water each—and there were ten of them! If a gallon of water weighs over eight pounds, Rebekah was doing a nightmare CrossFit/Orangetheory combo class of exertion, and she volunteered for it.

Abraham's servant presented Rebekah with costly gifts, to demonstrate his master's wealth, and he asked about staying with her family for the night. She graciously welcomed him to their home. Abraham's servant was on a mission and immediately rejoiced that God had blessed his efforts.

Then the man bowed down and worshiped the LORD, saying, "Praise be to the LORD, the God of my master Abraham, who has not abandoned his kindness and faithfulness to my master. As for me, the LORD has led me on the journey to the house of my master's relatives." (Genesis 24:26–27)

Rebekah ran back to her family to share the news. Her brother, Laban, was all too happy to welcome the generous stranger into their home. They rolled out the red carpet, washing the traveler's feet and those of the men with him, and set out a meal. But Abraham's trusted servant wouldn't eat until he'd told them exactly why he'd come so far. He wanted to take Rebekah back to Isaac, and he needed to know if her family would agree to the marriage. Her father and brother didn't hesitate.

> Laban and Bethuel answered, "This is from the LORD; we can say nothing to you one way or the other. Here is Rebekah; take her and go, and let her become the wife of your master's son, as the LORD has directed."
>
> When Abraham's servant heard what they said, he bowed down to the ground before the LORD. Then the servant brought out gold and silver jewelry and articles of clothing and gave them to Rebekah; he also gave costly gifts to her brother and to her mother. (Genesis 24:50–53)

It's almost beyond our comprehension how quickly this happened, and just how trusting Rebekah and her family were. They clearly saw God's hand in these events, though Rebekah's mother and brother tried to buy some time the next morning. They wanted another ten days with her, and what mother can't relate? *Just one more visit before you have to pack up for college! Just one more family dinner before you deploy!* But Abraham's servant urged them not to delay his return. In what appears to be an unusual twist, they said they'd ask Rebekah to decide. She consented to go along immediately, and her family sent her away with this blessing:

> Our sister, may you increase
>> to thousands upon thousands;
>> may your offspring possess
>> the cities of their enemies. (Genesis 24:60)

They traveled back to Isaac, who seemed thrilled with the match. Genesis 24:64 tells us about the moment Rebekah saw Isaac. The Hebrew translated literally is *vatipol me'al hagamal* or "fell off her camel." The Tree of Life version of the verse reads:

> Rebekah also lifted up her eyes and saw Isaac. Then she fell off her camel. (Genesis 24:46 TLV)

Was Rebekah so happy with what she saw in Isaac that she took a bit of a tumble? The end of Genesis 24 tells us simply, "She became his wife, and he loved her."

This love story was off to such a promising start! Rebekah was from the right family line, she was beautiful, she was hard-working, and she trusted in God's plan, despite having no advance warning or very many details about what's going to happen when she leaves behind her entire life as she's known it. To top it off, her new husband was prosperous *and* crazy about her.

There's such a beautiful parallel in what God the Father has done for each of you reading (or listening to) this book. Just like Abraham's son Isaac, a bride was prepared for Christ the Son. We the church are the bride, and like Rebekah, we were bought with a high price. We were sought out and brought into a new family. We are treasured and lavished with love. But that doesn't always mean that we're grateful or faithful. It's that part of us we see reflected in what eventually became of Rebekah.

REBEKAH THE WIFE AND MOTHER

Genesis 25:20 tells us Isaac was forty years old when he and Rebekah married. Just one verse later we learn that Rebekah was barren, and Isaac prayed for her. Remember, the Abrahamic covenant depended on Isaac's wife to have children who would become "a great nation." (Genesis 12:1–3) The pressure was on! God heard Isaac's pleas and Rebekah conceived. It's not until verse 26 that we learn Isaac was sixty when she finally gave birth! That's not an insignificant fact. Twenty years of waiting for motherhood, of Isaac's prayers and the delay in God's answer. What were those years like for this couple? Like Abraham, Isaac knew of God's promises about his descendants and what was to come. Was Isaac able to rest in that? What about Rebekah? We learn nothing about the conversations they had during those two decades of longing for a child.

When she finally became pregnant, Rebekah apparently didn't have an easy time of it. Long before ultrasound imaging, it's hard to imagine she could know twins were coming, but she was definitely having trouble. We see her go to God in prayer, asking for His explanation about her struggle. Rebekah and Isaac were living in Beer-lahai-roi at the time, the very place where Hagar (who was a servant of Abraham's wife and bore him his son Ishmael) encountered God while she was on the run. Beer-lahai-roi translates to "The Living One Who Sees Me," exactly what Hagar experienced when God connected with her in that place (Genesis 16:13–14). One generation later we witness Rebekah also going to God in turmoil, and hearing directly from Him.

The LORD said to her, "Two nations are in your womb, and two peoples from within you will be separated; one people will be stronger than the other, and the older will serve the younger." (Genesis 25:23)

After all that waiting, Rebekah learned that she was having two babies—and they were destined to be separated. It's easy to imagine that Rebekah thought any and all children she had would be part of the "great nation" that had been promised, but after God's revelation it seemed clear they would be two *different* nations. That couldn't have been easy to digest. God was declaring His sovereign choice of the younger over the older.

The boys grew up, and Esau became a skillful hunter, a man of the open country, while Jacob was content to stay at home among the tents. Isaac, who had a taste for wild game, loved Esau, but Rebekah loved Jacob. (Genesis 25:27–28)

These were obviously two very different boys, with two very different interests. It doesn't seem like Isaac and Rebekah did much to bridge the gap between the boys. What might have happened if the parents had simply accepted God's prophecy and worked together to prepare their sons for the future God had planned for them?

Rebekah was probably thrilled to have a child who wanted to share her world—who didn't mind hanging out with his mother and her servants in the tents. He would have been the child she could rely on to help her with chores, who learned the ways of managing a household, who slowly became her right hand. Rebekah had no more children after the twins, so there would be no daughter to share her world. It must have appeared like such a gift, to have this son who wanted to inhabit her world with her, who preferred her company to his father's or his brother's. Isaac's love for Esau too seemed to be about enjoying what his son could do for him.

It's hard to avoid the interpretation that these parents started using their children as their main emotional connection, instead of the connection they should have shared as spouses. As Isaac grew closer to Esau, and as Rebekah grew closer to Jacob, did a gulf grow between husband and wife? Here, Scripture shows us a picture of a truly unbalanced family, where the connection between husband and wife has been usurped by the connection between parent and child. It's easy to see how gradual that might have been, and how natural it might have seemed to both Isaac and Rebekah for a chasm to open between them as they both poured their emotional energy into the child they felt best reflected them individually.

And as much as Isaac loved Rebekah, we learn in Genesis 26 that Isaac wasn't above putting his wife in potential danger, as his father, Abraham, had done with his mother, Sarah. Just as Abraham had traveled in search of relief during a famine and wound up lying about his wife Sarah being his "sister," Isaac followed suit. During a later famine, Isaac and Rebekah also began to travel and God warned Isaac not to go into Egypt. He reminded Isaac of the oath He had made with Abraham and directed Isaac to settle in Gerar.

> When the men of that place asked him about his wife, he said, "She is my sister," because he was afraid to say, "She is my wife." He thought, "The men of this place might kill me on account of Rebekah, because she is beautiful."
>
> When Isaac had been there a long time, Abimelek king of the Philistines looked down from a window and saw Isaac caressing his wife Rebekah. So Abimelek summoned Isaac and said, "She is really your wife! Why did you say, 'She is my sister'?"
>
> Isaac answered him, "Because I thought I might lose my life on account of her." (Genesis 26:7–9)

Isaac repeated his father's cowardly action of lying to strangers, calling his wife his "sister" in order to preserve his own safety. How did Rebekah feel about being put in this position? We can only guess.

REBEKAH THE SCHEMER

When next we see Rebekah, some time has passed. Isaac's situation in the land had steadily improved. Unlike his father, Abraham, whose wealth derived purely from his flocks and whose roots were nomadic, Isaac stayed in one place long enough to become a farmer. Scripture tells us, "Isaac planted crops in that land and the same year reaped a hundredfold, because the LORD blessed him. The man became rich, and his wealth continued to grow until he became very wealthy" (Genesis 26:12–13). His relationships with the Philistines were guarded and respectful; they were clearly envious of this powerful and wealthy man, though King Abimelek cultivated friendly relations with Isaac (Genesis 26:1-22). But while the family's standing increased in the world, relationships within the family continued to deteriorate.

While Esau might've been bringing back all the hunting trophies, his twin brother Jacob (younger by a few minutes) was constantly looking for an edge. Ironically, Jacob was also a hunter, but Esau was his prey. Was the prophecy about the brothers' conflict in the back of his head? It's hard to believe Rebekah hadn't told her favored son about the word from God. Perhaps this is why as the differences between Jacob and Esau grew, Jacob jumped on the opportunity to exploit Esau in a moment of weakness.

Once when Jacob was cooking some stew, Esau came in from the open country, famished. He said to Jacob, "Quick, let me have some of that red stew! I'm famished!" (That is why he was also called Edom.) Jacob replied, "First sell me your birthright." "Look, I am about to die," Esau said. "What good is the birthright to me?"

But Jacob said, "Swear to me first." So he swore an oath to him, selling his birthright to Jacob. Then Jacob gave Esau some bread and some lentil stew. He ate and drank, and then got up and left. So Esau despised his birthright. (Genesis 25:29-34)

Why would Esau do such a thing, treating his inheritance so carelessly? The way he responded to Jacob's demand—"I am about to die. . . . What good is the birthright to me?"—shows that he was far more interested in satisfying his immediate physical hunger than in fulfilling his responsibility to the family. (And responsibility to *this* family, which was the beginning of Israel, was a bigger deal than to your average, everyday family.) Arrogant and unreflective, Esau let his cravings drive him into all sorts of rash decisions. Scripture says that his marriages to foreign women were already causing problems in the family, and may have contributed to Esau's unserious nature, for as the text says, he "despised his birthright" (Genesis 25:34). Though Jacob clearly leveraged this situation, Esau was not helpless. He's later called out in the book of Hebrews for so flippantly giving up something of such great value.

> See that no one is . . . godless like Esau, who for a single meal sold his inheritance rights as the oldest son. Afterward, as you know, when he wanted to inherit this blessing, he was rejected. Even though he sought the blessing with tears, he could not change what he had done. (Hebrews 12:16–17)

Esau made a terrible decision; that much is clear. But did his lapse justify the treachery that followed? And where was a parent to step in, before the rivalry between the brothers devolved to the point where there was no going back?

As it happens, a parent did get involved, but Rebekah's interference made things exponentially worse. At the age of 137, Isaac approached what he thought was the end of his life, and Rebekah wanted to ensure that her beloved Jacob would walk away with not only the birthright (guaranteeing a double portion of the inheritance), but also with the coveted blessing of his father as well.

When Isaac was old and his eyes were so weak that he could no longer see, he called for Esau, his older son, and said to him, "My son."

"Here I am," he answered.

Isaac said, "I am now an old man and don't know the day of my death. Now then, get your equipment—your quiver and bow—and go out to the open country to hunt some wild game for me. Prepare me the kind of tasty food I like and bring it to me to eat, so that I may give you my blessing before I die."

Now Rebekah was listening as Isaac spoke to his son Esau. When Esau left for the open country to hunt game and bring it back, Rebekah said to her son Jacob, "Look, I overheard your father say to your brother Esau, 'Bring me some game and prepare me some tasty food to eat, so that I may give you my blessing in the presence of the LORD before I die.' Now, my son, listen carefully and do what I tell you: Go out to the flock and bring me two choice young goats, so I can prepare some tasty food for your father, just the way he likes it. Then take it to your father to eat, so that he may give you his blessing before he dies." (Genesis 27:1-10)

What drove Rebekah to such appalling conduct? God Himself had told her that her younger son would be served by his older brother. Jacob had already conned Esau out of his birthright. Did Rebekah doubt that God would bring about what He had specifically told her? Was her faith so shallow that she thought she needed to give God some help?

Competitive mothers have made some notoriously terrible

decisions over the years. I'm reminded of a story I covered in 2021, involving a mother and daughter who allegedly schemed to make sure the seventeen-year-old would become her Florida high school's homecoming queen. Prosecutors say the mother, who was an assistant principal in the same school district, used her access to her employer's internal computer system to cast hundreds of phony votes in favor of her daughter. Both mother and daughter were charged with multiple felonies and faced up to sixteen years in jail. Both denied any wrongdoing. But the allegations spark the question: What would possess a mother to think abusing her position as a trusted school leader in order to rig a contest for her daughter was a wise decision? If convicted, I doubt either of them would say a rhinestone crown was worth destroying the young woman's future and potentially landing them both behind bars.

The young woman in that case was charged as an adult. Just like her, Jacob was his own person, but in both cases their mothers had an enormous, negative influence on their children. When parents' mistakes—large or small—have unintended consequences, do they bear the weight of that as well? At what point are adult children responsible for their own actions? Even if Jacob did act entirely on his own in the matter of the birthright, his mother had certainly done nothing to encourage an apology or to discourage Jacob's rivalry with his brother. Rebekah actually took it a step further, easily manipulating Jacob, who was then seventy-seven years old, to follow her deceptive lead.

In the end, the issue is not *how responsible we are for our children's actions,* but *what we've done to help our children face and weather the consequences of those actions.* It appears Rebekah taught her son how to evade the fallout. Because of that, he never really became responsible until he had left home and escaped his mother's influence. But at that moment in Genesis 27 their worst deception was still unfolding.

> Jacob said to Rebekah his mother, "But my brother Esau is a hairy man while I have smooth skin. What if my father touches me? I would appear to be tricking him and would bring down a curse on myself rather than a blessing." (Genesis 27:11-12)

Oh, okay! So, Jacob wasn't concerned about scamming his dying father. No, he was more worried he might be cursed by accident.

Here's where we really see Rebekah go off the rails.

> His mother said to him, "My son, let the curse fall on me. Just do what I say; go and get them for me."
> So he went and got them and brought them to his mother, and she prepared some tasty food, just the way his father liked it. Then Rebekah took the best clothes of Esau her older son, which she had in the house, and put them on her younger son Jacob. She also covered his hands and the smooth part of his neck with the goatskins. Then she handed to her son Jacob the tasty food and the bread she had made. (Genesis 27:13-17)

The extent to which Rebekah had taken over Jacob's moral agency here is stark and disturbing. "Let the curse fall on me," she said, again telegraphing that she was willing to take on any risk in order to ensure that her favored son came out on top. *She* went and got Esau's clothing. *She* doctored the goatskins and fitted them to Jacob's hands and neck. *She* made the food to take to Isaac. Rebekah plotted every step of this deceptive scheme, and she asked only that Jacob obey her and follow her lead. It appears she'd so stunted his own emotional growth that Jacob was putty in her hands—a docile puppet.

Mothers have incredible sway over their children, but when they become obsessed with manipulating everything that stands in the way of the future they imagine for that child, no good can come from it. It's tempting. Just look at the college admissions scandal that blew up in 2019. The law enforcement operation that busted up the scheme was dubbed Operation Varsity Blues. Some very prominent mothers were among those arrested, charged, and jailed. In some cases their children didn't know about the fake test scores or phony college applications. In others, the children knew and were full participants. How much damage is done when a child follows the lead of a mother he or she trusts to have their best interests at heart, when the end game is nothing but an elaborate web of deception? It ripples through a lifetime, and sometimes for generations.

Let's not lose sight of Isaac in this narrative. He was old and blind, and it's possible his memory and mind were fading too. Despite those challenges, when Jacob came to his father clad in his crude goatskin costume, Isaac sensed something was off.

[Jacob] went to his father and said, "My father."

"Yes, my son," he answered. "Who is it?"

Jacob said to his father, "I am Esau your firstborn. I have done as you told me. Please sit up and eat some of my game, so that you may give me your blessing."

Isaac asked his son, "How did you find it so quickly, my son?"

"The LORD your God gave me success," he replied. (Genesis 27:18–20)

Okay, this is the exact moment where I'd start to worry about getting struck by lightning. Rebekah and Jacob were all in on this shameful plan to deceive—not just some random old man—but their own husband and father. About to be exposed, Jacob invoked the name of God Himself to cover his deceitful tracks. We grieve our heavenly Father when we sin, but to invoke His name in the process? It's a clue to just how far Jacob was from worship and commitment to God that he could so blithely drag God's name into his schemes.

Isaac still had questions.

Then Isaac said to Jacob, "Come near so I can touch you, my son, to know whether you really are my son Esau or not."

Jacob went close to his father Isaac, who touched him and said, "The voice is the voice of Jacob, but the hands are the hands of Esau." He did not recognize him, for his hands were hairy like those of his brother Esau; so he proceeded to bless him. "Are you really my son Esau?" he asked.

"I am," he replied. (Genesis 27:18–24)

There is a calculated cruelty to this scene. How did Rebekah get to the place where she was unabashedly willing to betray her aging husband, even as his faculties were failing him? We see in earlier passages that Rebekah had long since abandoned her emotional loyalty to Isaac in favor of her connection with her son. Had Isaac done the same with regard to Esau? How had this family, which started with such a promising love story, devolved into a bad soap opera plot?

It seems Isaac and Rebekah had turned away from each other, in order to focus exclusively on their children. As we have seen, each allowed his or her relationship with a favored child to become the most important one, instead of the spousal connection. The impulse to push aside the spouse and elevate the child is nothing new to our culture; it's as old as human civilization. But the Bible warns us here about the very real risks of doing that—dangers to the emotional and moral development of the children, to the marriage, and to the happiness and stability of the entire family.

Finally, Rebekah got to the point of treating her husband with such contempt that at his most vulnerable, she saw him as nothing more than an object to be manipulated, one more thing to be used to further the advantage of the person she actually cared most about: her son. Much as our society often communicates to parents that there is nothing more important than focusing on their children, the Bible reminds us that the best way to give children the love and support they need is by first giving it to our spouse and modeling a healthy marriage.

In the end, Isaac was persuaded by Jacob's lies and lavished him with a generous and beautiful blessing.

Then he said, "My son, bring me some of your game to eat, so that I may give you my blessing."
Jacob brought it to him and he ate; and he brought

some wine and he drank. Then his father Isaac said to him, "Come here, my son, and kiss me."

So he went to him and kissed him. When Isaac caught the smell of his clothes, he blessed him and said,

"Ah, the smell of my son
is like the smell of a field
that the LORD has blessed.
May God give you heaven's dew
and earth's richness
an abundance of grain and new wine.
May nations serve you
and peoples bow down to you.
Be lord over your brothers,
and may the sons of your mother bow down to you."
(Genesis 27:25-29)

Did Rebekah hear any of this exchange? Was she leaning in at the tent door to listen? It's easy to picture her eavesdropping on the entire exchange with glee, thrilled that her devious scheme had finally cemented every possible benefit to Jacob and his future.

Once Jacob left, one of the most gut-wrenching scenes in all of the Bible played out. An unaware Esau went for his blessing, at once discovering the shock of what had just happened and almost certainly breaking Isaac's heart as the depths of the betrayal he'd suffered at the hands of his own son began to sink in.

After Isaac finished blessing him, and Jacob had scarcely left his father's presence, his brother Esau came in from hunting. He too prepared some tasty food and brought it to his father. Then he said to him, "My father, please sit up and eat some of my game, so that you may give me your blessing."

His father Isaac asked him, "Who are you?"

"I am your son," he answered, "your firstborn, Esau."

Isaac trembled violently and said, "Who was it, then, that hunted game and brought it to me? I ate it just before you came and I blessed him—and indeed he will be blessed!"

When Esau heard his father's words, he burst out with a loud and bitter cry and said to his father, "Bless me—me too, my father!"

But he said, "Your brother came deceitfully and took your blessing." (Genesis 27:30-35)

Desperate, enraged, and panicked, Esau begged for some shred of blessing from his devastated father. In those times, once the blessing was spoken, it was basically as binding as a contract. Esau knew his entire life had been ransacked. He'd already willingly given away his birthright. But as the older brother, Esau was probably banking on the fact that he'd still have Isaac's blessing in the end. The crushing reality that the blessing was gone too was a shock to Esau's system.

Esau lashed out, pointing to the very origins of the twins' dispute. As Esau was being born, Jacob was literally clinging to his foot (Genesis 25:26). Jacob's name literally means "grasps the heel"—a Hebrew expression for deception. As the devastating reality of Jacob's latest duplicity was settling in on Esau he invoked that history.

Esau said, "Isn't he rightly named Jacob? This is the second time he has taken advantage of me: He took my birthright, and now he's taken my blessing!" (Genesis 27:36)

Let's not forget Esau's own role in giving up his birthright. Did Jacob take advantage? Yes, but Esau was flippant and careless with something he should have valued much more highly. That was Esau's choice. This matter with regard to Isaac's dying blessing was not.

Now picture Isaac, deceived and manipulated by his closest family members and left with almost nothing to give his beloved son.

Esau said to his father, "Do you have only one blessing, my father? Bless me too, my father!" Then Esau wept aloud.
His father Isaac answered him,

"Your dwelling will be
away from the earth's richness,
away from the dew of heaven above.
You will live by the sword
and you will serve your brother.
But when you grow restless,
you will throw his yoke
from off your neck."

Esau held a grudge against Jacob because of the blessing his father had given him. He said to himself, "The days of mourning for my father are near; then I will kill my brother Jacob." (Genesis 27:38–41)

If it was possible to think of Esau as the irresponsible, negligent villain before—the mindless brute his brother probably saw—that version of Esau was gone. It seems he finally understood what Jacob had taken from him. Esau "burst out with a loud and bitter cry," the Bible tells us, and he "wept aloud" (Genesis 27:34, 38). How can we not feel some measure of sympathy for this man who has been outwitted at every turn by his brother—and now by his own mother? In this enormously complicated story, even the bad guys don't stay the bad guys. By the end of the story, our sympathy for Jacob has nearly evaporated.

What of Rebekah, in the aftermath of all this, when she learned that Esau planned to murder his own brother?

> When Rebekah was told what her older son Esau had said, she sent for her younger son Jacob and said to him, "Your brother Esau is planning to avenge himself by killing you. Now then, my son, do what I say: Flee at once to my brother Laban in Harran. Stay with him for a while until your brother's fury subsides. When your brother is no longer angry with you and forgets what you did to him, I'll send word for you to come back from there. Why should I lose both of you in one day?" (Genesis 27:42–45)

We can observe two key things here. Rebekah was acknowledging that she'd lost Esau. She had to have made that calculation already, but now the reality of what she'd done to her oldest son had arrived. Their relationship was forever scarred. The second impact of her sin meant that she'd have to send Jacob away—the son she cherished because he was the one who spent his time with her, in the tents and doing what she valued. How ironic in that exploiting every possible angle for Jacob's advantage, she'd essentially lost him too.

Rebekah wasn't done with her conniving just yet. Having betrayed Isaac, she took things yet another step further. When she should have been confessing her role in the whole scam and begging for forgiveness, Rebekah instead took the opportunity to both complain about Esau's wives and to once again mislead Isaac.

Then Rebekah said to Isaac, "I'm disgusted with living because of these Hittite women. If Jacob takes a wife from among the women of this land, from Hittite women like these, my life will not be worth living." (Genesis 27:42–46)

Rebekah doubled down on her lies and went from one deception to another. Instead of telling her husband the real reason why she wanted to get Jacob out of town quickly, she made up a plausible reason for sending him away to her brother, Laban. Isaac, of course, was aware of the deception practiced on him, but it is unclear if he had discovered yet that Rebekah was the source of it. Isaac had told Esau that "your brother came deceitfully and stole your blessing" (Genesis 27:35), but he did not name Rebekah, and possibly he did not realize—or did not want to realize—that his own wife was behind what had happened to Esau *and* to him. But relations between them must have been strained. She could have just said to Isaac, *We have to get Jacob away because Esau is planning on killing him,* but after everything that had happened, perhaps she was worried Isaac wouldn't stop Esau's plans for revenge.

This is the last passage in which Rebekah appears; she does

not say another word in the Bible. Jacob sets off on his journey to Laban's family, and he winds up the victim of some rather poetic justice. What Jacob encountered on that journey was likely far more than he had ever imagined. Remember, when Jacob was deceiving his own father, he invoked God's name in support of the scheme. Note *how* he phrased it. Jacob told Isaac that "the Lord your God gave me success" (Genesis 27:20). It is a small but telling detail that Jacob did not say "the Lord *our* God," but "the Lord *your* God." God was removed from Jacob's concerns—a matter for his father to worry about, but not him. It was only when Jacob left his home (and his mother's manipulation) far behind him that he was able to finally become who he was destined to be. It was only once he'd separated from that family dysfunction that Jacob encountered the living God.

Both Jacob and Esau had a lot of growing up to do, once free of the influence of their parents. In the wilderness, Jacob had repeated encounters with God. Many years later he even wrestled with "a man" (Jacob's description of the encounter in Genesis 32:30—"I saw God face to face"—has led some to believe this was God Himself) to the point he was left with a limp. But as a result of that hand-to-hand combat, Jacob was given a new name: Israel, meaning, "he strives with God." Jacob had finally received a blessing from a different Father, a blessing he obtained by sheer stubbornness. God had chosen Jacob before he was born as part of His master plan.

And what of Esau, who years before was left in despair and disinheritance? Just because Jacob was the chosen one, did that mean Esau was lost forever? The granting of the name Israel to Jacob was paralleled in Scripture by a blessing that Jacob *really* didn't see coming. After his supernatural wrestling match, Jacob soon encountered Esau again after all those years of separation and bad blood. Petrified by the memory of Esau's anger, Jacob tried to buy his brother's favor by sending ahead gifts of herds. But look at what happened when they finally met:

> Jacob looked up and there was Esau, coming with his four hundred men; so he divided the children among Leah, Rachel and the two female servants. He put the female servants and their children in front, Leah and her children next, and Rachel and Joseph in the rear. He himself went on ahead and bowed down to the ground seven times as he approached his brother.
>
> But Esau ran to meet Jacob and embraced him; he threw his arms around his neck and kissed him. And they wept . . .
>
> Esau asked, "What's the meaning of all these flocks and herds I met?"
>
> "To find favor in your eyes, my lord," he said.
>
> But Esau said, "I already have plenty, my brother. Keep what you have for yourself." (Genesis 33:1-4, 8-9)

Who was *this*? Esau had had a complete change of heart. After the years "away from the earth's richness, away from the dew of heaven above . . . liv[ing] by the sword," which Isaac had prophesied for his older son (Genesis 27:39-40), Esau finally did "throw [Jacob's] yoke from off [his] neck" (Genesis 39:40)—which took the very unexpected form of throwing off his hatred for his brother.

Esau had discarded a burden of anger and struggle and joyfully embraced his twin brother—the same brother who had stolen his favored role right out from under him. What a beautiful, if brief, moment of harmony in this troubled family. Jacob must have found it difficult to believe—in fact, he was still so hesitant that he moved his herds into pagan lands instead of fully reconciling himself to his brother. Still, it's a lovely picture of forgiveness. God would later instruct the Israelites not to "despise" the descendants of Esau, because they were family (Deuteronomy 23:7).

What would Jacob's and Esau's lives have been like if they had not been divided by their parents' favoritism—and Rebekah's destructive trickery? Perhaps their reconciliation could have come much sooner. Esau's redemption beautifully illustrates how, with humility and repentance, even the worst betrayals can be overcome. This brotherly reunion came despite their mother's efforts, not because of them. Selfish to the end, Rebekah had told Jacob that he needed to flee Esau's wrath so that she would not lose both her sons in one day. She saw the consequences only through the lens of what would happen to her, and she focused solely on her own potential grief and sorrow. She was blind to Isaac's anguish, and to Esau's, and even to Jacob's as well. She had seen in Jacob a receptacle for her own hopes and dreams, and she had pushed him to become who she desired him to be. Rebekah assumed that if Jacob was going to get ahead, it was up to her. She refused to surrender her child's well-being to God. She was unwilling to let His promises come to fruition without her meddling. Far too many of us are tempted to dabble with this path, instead of trusting in God's unwavering ability to accomplish what He's promised.

Rebekah's father-in-law, Abraham, had literally been willing to surrender his own beloved son to God when he believed God was asking him to sacrifice Isaac on an altar. Abraham had been willing to trust God beyond what most of us can imagine. Abraham knew God would fulfill His promises to preserve Abraham's descendants, even if that would mean raising Isaac from the dead. Despite having received a divine promise about her son's blessed destiny, Rebekah was Abraham's opposite. She clutched her son close, not showing any faith in God's promises. In the end, Jacob wound up meeting God only after leaving his mother behind. By nearly smothering Jacob, Rebekah wound up losing him.

In the Gospel of John, Jesus tells us that "anyone who loves their life will lose it, while anyone who hates their life in this world will keep it for eternal life" (John 12:25). The same principle can be true of one of God's most treasured gifts: children. When mothers let their desires and plans and schemes take priority over what God has planned for their children, they forget that the sacred vocation of motherhood requires giving to God what was always His. When mothers selflessly guide their children to figure out what God has mapped out for their lives, they can rest in knowing that they are fulfilling their purpose as parents as well. It's only human to experience apprehension, but we know God is good and is always working His plans to the good of those who love Him and are called for His purposes (Romans 8:28).

Lord God, grant mothers the courage to surrender their children to You. Help them to place their own hopes and dreams for their precious children into Your hands, committing them to Your perfect will. We ask that You direct the love of our families in the right way, and to the holiest of purposes. Help us all to honor Your designs for marriage. Give mothers around the world the strength to recognize that their own plans for their children can never be better than what You have in store for them, in Your infinite wisdom and compassion.

Rebekah Study Questions

1. Why was Abraham so firm about where Isaac's wife should come from? (Genesis 24:1–9) What covenant promises were prophesied to flow through Isaac? Contrast this with Esau's choice of wives later in this story. (Genesis 26:34; 27:46; Genesis 28:8–9)

2. What process did Abraham's servant undertake in looking for a wife for Isaac, and how did God answer his prayers? (Genesis 24:10–27). How do you approach a difficult task when the prospect seems overwhelming?

3. Rebekah and Isaac's love story got off to such a promising start, followed by twenty years of infertility and then a difficult pregnancy. How do you think God's prophecy regarding Rebekah's unborn children impacted her and Isaac as parents? (Genesis 25:23)

4. What did the birthright mean to sons in ancient times, and who do you feel was more to blame about what happened between Jacob and Esau in Genesis 25:27–33? What does the interaction tell you about each of the sons?

5. Did Isaac set the example of deception for his family? (Genesis 26:7–11) What was the possible message that sent to Rebekah and their sons?

6. Why was Rebekah willing to betray her husband in such a way? (Genesis 27:1–46) What does it say about her faith in God and His promises? How much responsibility does Jacob bear?

BATHSHEBA

(1 Samuel 11–12, Psalm 51, 1 Kings 1–3:15)

If the name Bathsheba immediately conjures in your mind the image of a scheming seductress who trapped a king into an illicit affair, you're not alone. Like me, you probably saw her Sunday school flannelgraph character gazing over her shoulder with a come-hither look in her eyes. I mean, it was as racy as those storyboards got! Maybe you've learned more about Bathsheba over time as you read the Scriptures for yourself, and you know she's not that one-dimensional woman so easily judged and cast aside. If you're still undecided, I ask you to come with me on a journey to get to know this woman better, to see what the Bible tells us about her extraordinary life—one that changed the course of human history.

BATHSHEBA THE GRIEVING WIDOW

From the moment we're introduced to Bathsheba in 2 Samuel 11, something is already out of whack. We're told it was "in the spring at the time when kings march out to war" (2 Samuel 11:1), but that King David had not gone along with his army, as he had so many times in the past. Why? I don't know, but staying in Jerusalem gave the king time to get up from his bed one evening and stroll around the palace rooftop. At that hour and from that perch, he saw a "very beautiful woman" bathing herself (2 Samuel 11:2). The Bible gives no indication that Bathsheba thought anyone could see her or that she was attempting to attract attention at that late hour in the space where she bathed privately. In reality, she was fulfilling scriptural requirements for cleansing herself. Here's what happened next:

> David sent someone to find out about her. The man said, "She is Bathsheba, the daughter of Eliam and the wife of Uriah the Hittite." (2 Samuel 11:3)

It's almost as if the person sent to gather intel on this attractive woman was providing David both information *and* a warning. *She's married... and you know her family.* Time for a little background. In 2 Samuel 23 we find that David knew plenty about Bathsheba's husband. Uriah the Hittite was part of an elite band of thirty "chief warriors" who protected David and fought on his behalf.

We don't know how a Hittite came to be one of the king's most trusted officers and a loyal soldier of Israel, but it might have had something to do with Bathsheba. Did Uriah convert to the Jewish faith because he fell in love with her? It is probable that Uriah was not the name he was born with, because Uriah is a Hebrew name meaning "the Lord is my light." Whoever he was, we know Uriah had made a choice to be who and where he was—and presumably Bathsheba was part of that choice.

Despite his personal relationship with Uriah, David showed zero hesitation when provided with the details about Bathsheba.

> Then David sent messengers to get her. She came to him, and he slept with her. (2 Samuel 11:4)

That escalated quickly! We have no way of knowing what conversation they may or may not have had, but let's keep the enormous power differential in mind. The army of Israel, which included Bathsheba's husband Uriah, was away in battle on behalf of the king, and she was summoned to the palace. King David's call was not the sort of invitation she could likely refuse.

Put yourself in Bathsheba's shoes for a moment. She was a military wife. Maybe she thought there was news of Uriah. Her heart must have been in her throat as she hurried to the palace, apprehensive about what news awaited her there. Imagine her response when it turned out the news was that King David wanted to sleep with her. Was she flattered? Was she terrified for herself, for the price her loved ones might pay if she refused? The Bible doesn't tell us much, and we don't fully know what her options were in this situation; but it is clear that David, the king, was far more responsible for the sinful fling than the woman who was his subject. We're told Bathsheba returned home after David had what he wanted. She soon learned she was pregnant and then sent word to the palace.

At this point, King David held all the cards. I wonder how frightened Bathsheba must have been in those agonizing days and weeks, realizing she was carrying a child who was clearly not her husband's. She could have been stoned for adultery. Uriah would have been justified in casting her aside completely. Unwilling to take responsibility for his sin, David decided to add to his growing list of transgressions. He plotted to bring Uriah home from the battlefront, in hopes that the brave warrior would sleep with his wife and believe the child to be his own. So David sent word to his top commander, Joab: "Send me Uriah the Hittite" (2 Samuel 11:6). Once Uriah arrived at the palace, David warmly greeted him and then sent him home to Bathsheba with a gift.

> But Uriah slept at the entrance to the palace with all his master's servants and did not go down to his house. (2 Samuel 11:9)

Uh-oh. David, you have a problem. Knowing his plan was crumbling, the king called in Uriah to explain why he didn't go.

> Uriah said to David, "The ark and Israel and Judah are staying in tents, and my commander Joab and my lord's men are camped in the open country. How could I go to my house to eat and drink and make love to my wife? As surely as you live, I will not do such a thing!" (2 Samuel 11:11)

Many scholars who study this time period say the army would likely have been under strict protocols during this battle to remain abstinent. Even though Uriah was brought back to his beautiful wife and the comforts of home, he refused to compromise his integrity. David compelled him to stay another day, and he even got him drunk that night. Still, Uriah resisted whatever pull he must have experienced to go to his own house.

This is yet another inflection point. David had slept with someone else's wife, impregnated her, and then hatched a ruse to make her husband believe the child was his. Enough cars had piled onto the growing wreckage, but there's nothing in Scripture that suggests David even *thought* about confessing and beginning the cleanup mission. Instead, he sent his loyal warrior Uriah away, carrying his own death warrant.

In the morning David wrote a letter to Joab and sent it with Uriah. In it he wrote, "Put Uriah out in front where the fighting is fiercest. Then withdraw from him so he will be struck down and die." (2 Samuel 11:15)

Let that sink in: the plot to murder an honorable man, cooked up by the king himself. Uriah was such a devoted soldier that David didn't hesitate to ask him to deliver this confidential letter, which contained instructions for ending Uriah's life, because David knew Uriah would never pierce the seal of secrecy.

As we see David's treachery grow, we learn nothing about how Bathsheba was coping. Did she have any clue what the king was up to? Did she even know Uriah had been in town? It's hard to imagine that word of her husband's unexpected visit hadn't made its way to her. If she heard Uriah was at the palace, she probably figured out that David was trying desperately to cover his tracks. But we see no communication between Bathsheba and the king as he sets his homicidal plan in motion.

So while Joab had the city under siege, he put Uriah at a place where he knew the strongest defenders were. When the men of the city came out and fought against Joab, some of the men in David's army fell; moreover, Uriah the Hittite died. (2 Samuel 11:16–17)

Take note: not only was Uriah killed, but the Bible also tells us others lost their lives as part of David's deadly scheme. His plan led to multiple innocent casualties as Joab was forced to send his troops to undertake a risky and pointless action just to disguise Uriah's murder. When word of the deaths reached David, he didn't crumple in guilt and shame. Instead, he directed a messenger to tell Joab:

> Don't let this upset you; the sword devours one as well as another. (2 Samuel 11:25)

This man who was anointed and chosen by God, who rose from shepherd boy to celebrated king, had become something nearly unrecognizable: an adulterer and a murderer, cold-blooded, calculating, and wicked beyond words. But God has a way of making sure our sins do not remain hidden. Bathsheba's chaotic world was about to get much worse.

> When Uriah's wife heard that her husband was dead, she mourned for him. After the time of mourning was over, David had her brought to his house, and she became his wife and bore him a son. But the thing David had done displeased the LORD. (2 Samuel 11:26-27)

What a chilling statement. David was in serious trouble. We see throughout Scripture how God deals with those who violate His commands and His trust. As the man handpicked to lead the nation of Israel, David had once been humble and totally reliant on God. Let this be a bright red warning flag to every one of us. Just because we have walked closely with our heavenly Father, trusting Him through impossible challenges and seeing His faithfulness over and over again, does not mean we cannot fall into grievous sin. Our sin rarely starts with adultery and murder, but it begins when we allow our hearts and minds to be distracted and drawn away, even by things that are essentially good. When our ego is flattered or our attention diverted, the tiniest seeds begin to be planted, which will sprout into full-grown weeds. I often find myself due for a good round of weeding when I've allowed things other than the Lord to strip my attention away from Him. As with any garden, weeding out sin isn't a single round of maintenance. It's a lifelong work of tending and trimming and discarding what isn't good fruit.

At what point did the field of David's heart become so overgrown with sin? And what about Bathsheba? We still don't know what she was feeling or thinking through any of this, only that she was once again summoned to the palace for an offer it's unlikely she had autonomy to refuse: marriage to the king.

At this point, David may have thought he'd finally extinguished the wildfire of sin he launched on that rooftop walk months earlier, but it's impossible to forget the scorched earth it left behind. God certainly hadn't, and He was about to show up and pronounce judgment on David via Nathan the prophet.

As 2 Samuel 12 begins, God has revealed the truth to Nathan, who then confronted the king.

When he came to him, he said, "There were two men in a certain town, one rich and the other poor. The rich man had a very large number of sheep and cattle, but the poor man had nothing except one little ewe lamb he had bought. He raised it, and it grew up with him and his children. It shared his food, drank from his cup and even slept in his arms. It was like a daughter to him.

Now a traveler came to the rich man, but the rich man refrained from taking one of his own sheep or cattle to prepare a meal for the traveler who had come to him.

Instead, he took the ewe lamb that belonged to the poor man and prepared it for the one who had come to him. (2 Samuel 12:1-4)

Nathan's story of injustice and cruelty evokes all kinds of emotions, from grief to anger. What arrogance for a man who has so much to take the one adored, loved possession from someone who has little else! Not surprisingly, David saw it the same way.

David burned with anger against the man and said to Nathan, "As surely as the LORD lives, the man who did this must die! He must pay for that lamb four times over, because he did such a thing and had no pity." (2 Samuel 12:5-6)

And *this* is the one moment in the Bible that, whenever I read it, I can't get one particularly saucy daytime talk show out of my head. It's like I can hear Nathan yelling, "You *are* the father!" But it doesn't go exactly like that. . . .

Then Nathan said to David, "You are the man! This is what the LORD, the God of Israel, says: 'I anointed you king over Israel, and I delivered you from the hand of Saul. I gave your master's house to you, and your master's wives into your arms. I gave you all Israel and Judah. And if all this had been too little, I would have given you even more. Why did you despise the word of the LORD by doing what is evil in his eyes? You struck down Uriah the Hittite with the sword and took his wife to be your own. You killed him with the sword of the Ammonites. Now, therefore, the sword will never depart from your house, because you despised me and took the wife of Uriah the Hittite to be your own.'

"This is what the LORD says: 'Out of your own household I am going to bring calamity on you. Before your very eyes I will take your wives and give them to one who is close to you, and he will sleep with your wives in broad daylight. You did it in secret, but I will do this thing in broad daylight before all Israel.'" (2 Samuel 12:7-12)

Like so many of us, David had assumed that in the story of his life, he was the hero, the good guy, the one who loved God and tried to do what was right. But without noticing it, David had become the rich man in Nathan's parable—heedless of others, careless with people's lives, treating the less fortunate as objects to be used and expended at will. He had let his army go off to war without him, and he had spent his free time ravishing the wife of a war comrade. He'd arranged an honorable man's murder, and in the process betrayed even more of his loyal soldiers who fought to put him on the throne. Despite his riches, he stole from a man of integrity.

How agonizing that must have been for David to realize what he had become! Remember, he'd once been identified as "a man after God's own heart" (1 Samuel 13:14). David's repentance was immediate and profound. Nathan assured the king that his sin had been forgiven by God, but he warned David that God's punishment would be incredibly painful. David's betrayal of the marriage bond between Bathsheba and Uriah meant that his own wives and concubines would be betrayed into the hands of someone else—as indeed happened, when his son Absalom violated the king's concubines in the sight of all Jerusalem. But in the more immediate future, Nathan told David that the child he had conceived with Bathsheba would die. David spent days pleading for the child's life, weeping, mourning, fasting, and begging.

For all his sins—and they were many—David also experienced extraordinary closeness to the Lord. Maybe it was because he had known such sin in his life that he eventually came to understand the mercy and love of the Lord in an even deeper way. Whatever David did, he did with his whole heart—fighting, loving, sinning, praying, repenting. Even after he heard the verdict of God from the mouth of the prophet Nathan, he refused to give up. He knew well the merciful nature of God, and he held on to the hope that while there was life in his son's body, there was a chance the dreadful verdict could be turned aside. So David gave himself completely over to prayer. Yet Nathan's prophecy proved true, and the boy died.

The child of David and Bathsheba is not given a name at any point in this story, and we don't see Bathsheba's experience as this tragedy is unfolding. As readers, we are left with the question: What did Bathsheba know about any of this? It could be that until Nathan's public reproach of the king, and David's public repentance, Bathsheba had no idea about the circumstances of her husband's death. It must have been devastating, either way. Her current husband was revealed to be a liar and a murderer, and her precious and innocent child, who had nothing to do with any of the decisions of his parents, suffered because of it. The thought of Bathsheba's suffering here is almost unbearable. In the case of Bathsheba, we have to resort to some guessing about what she must have been thinking about David. But the grief of watching your only child waste away in a sickness that you can't stop, in cries that you can't soothe, is a universally understood human emotion.

We live in a world that finds grief troublesome, embarrassing. We don't live with death every day, the way our ancestors did. We don't wash and clothe our own dead anymore; we don't keep vigil over their bodies for days. In our culture, the reality of death exists at a distance from us—and some of that is a good thing! The problem is that when death is separated from the practical reality of our lives, grief can become something strange, unnatural, almost shameful. When we see someone overcome with grief, maybe sobbing, too often our reaction is embarrassment. Or worse, we may think that an extravagant display of grief means a lack of faith.

For many of us, it's not easy to be vulnerable when we're struggling. I remember after my father died suddenly, I felt like I'd been thrown into a parallel universe that no one else was inhabiting. Financial matters were left unresolved, court battles bubbled up, and I felt like I didn't have time to grieve. There was too much else to do, and when people asked how I was doing, it was easier to say, "Well, I know I'll see him again one day" than to unload the tidal wave of grief I felt might drown me. I distinctly remember being on the treadmill at the gym trying to hold it together and thinking, *The person bouncing along next to me has no idea I just lost my dad and I might completely lose it any second.* As a Christian, I worried that falling apart might telegraph that my faith was weak.

But grief is a good and healthy reaction to a fallen world. Our grief tells God that we cherish His gifts to us—we cherish them so much that we sometimes can't imagine our lives without them. Our pain tells God how much we value life. Too often mothers who lose their children—especially mothers who lose their babies before they are even born—feel they need to hide their anguish.

I don't for a second think God asks that of us. Who better understands the grief of watching a child suffer and die than our own heavenly Father? He has suffered as we do, and He will meet us in our grief. Psalms urges us, "Cast your cares on the LORD and he will sustain you; he will never let the righteous be shaken" (55:22) and reminds us "The LORD is close to the brokenhearted" (34:18).

I think this is an important spot for a bit of a biblical rabbit hole. I've often found comfort in the words David wrote in Psalm 51, when he was begging for God's forgiveness. As I suspected, experts believe this psalm was written after he was confronted by Nathan with the gravity of what he'd done. He pleaded for mercy, admitted the depth of his sin, and accepted that the Lord's verdict against him was just and true.

> Create in me a pure heart, O God,
>   and renew a steadfast spirit within me.
>   Do not cast me from your presence
>   or take your Holy Spirit from me.
>   Restore to me the joy of your salvation
>   and grant me a willing spirit, to sustain me. . . .
>   You do not delight in sacrifice, or I would bring it;
>   you do not take pleasure in burnt offerings.
>   My sacrifice, O God, is a broken spirit;
>   a broken and contrite heart
>   you, God, will not despise. (Psalm 51:10–12, 16–17)

David was broken. Have you been there? I sure have, left only with the remnants of my selfish choices and guilt over those I wounded. Few of us will ever weave a web as tangled and deadly as David did, but it's likely all of us will have regrets over some of our sinful choices. Take heart, there is redemption. No matter how minor or monstrous our transgressions, God's forgiveness is ours for the asking (Psalm 103:12).

We see after the child's death that David pulled himself together and "went into the house of the LORD and worshiped" (2 Samuel 12:20). This is also the first glimpse we have of any tenderness between David and Bathsheba. Rather than casting her away as someone he no longer needed around,

> Then David comforted his wife Bathsheba, and he went to her and made love to her. She gave birth to a son, and they named him Solomon. The LORD loved him. (2 Samuel 12:24)

Perhaps in this we can see their reconciliation, and Bathsheba's forgiveness of her husband. For the first time, maybe, they have come to understand each other. The name they gave their little boy means "peace."

Let's take stock of Bathsheba's story to this point: summoned by the king for his pleasure, then sent home. Pregnant with a child who was not her husband's, widowed, married to the king, and then stripped of her child. Finally, some joy in her life with the arrival of Solomon. In a movie, this might be where the credits would roll and they'd all live happily ever after. In this case? Not a chance, but it *is* the beginning of a new life for Bathsheba, one that will give her back her voice in the palaces of David.

BATHSHEBA THE MOTHER OF ISRAEL

If you've spent much time in church or studying the Bible you've heard of Bathsheba and you've heard of Solomon, but you may not have realized their connection. This is the part of Bathsheba's story when we discover her enormous influence in shaping the nation of Israel. Bathsheba is also only one of a handful of women referenced in the lineage of Christ (Matthew 1:6). All of this telegraphs to us that she isn't just a footnote in David's story, but a woman who came to be a power player in her own right.

Solomon was not the oldest of David's sons, but it appears he had favor with his father from the beginning. And when it came to advocating for her son, Bathsheba was a lioness. No longer a grieving young woman, she learned to navigate royal politics all too well. That skill cemented Solomon's place on the throne, but not without some serious challenges.

When we meet up with Bathsheba again in 1 Kings 1, David is fading. He's so old and frail his servants searched the kingdom for a beautiful young woman, and they found Abishag to keep him warm by sleeping beside him, though the Bible tells us there was no sexual relationship. The king was no longer young and virile, so the race to replace him was on.

Leading the pack was his son Adonijah, whose mother was Haggith. We're told in 1 Kings 1:5 Adonijah kept putting himself forward and saying, "I will be king!" He pulled together chariots and dozens of men to run ahead of him. We also get a couple more nuggets: he was "very handsome" (1 Kings 1:6), and David had never rebuked or chastised him over his behavior. Adonijah was also quite a schemer, conspiring with David's one-time military master, Joab. Working to lay his claim to the throne, Adonijah sacrificed scores of animals and invited people from all over the kingdom to join him. Guess who he left off the guest list?

But he did not invite Nathan the prophet or Benaiah or the special guard or his brother Solomon. (1 Kings 1:10)

And it's not like they weren't going to hear about the massive party!

Nathan wasn't going down without a fight:

Then Nathan asked Bathsheba, Solomon's mother, "Have you not heard that Adonijah, the son of Haggith, has become king, and our lord David knows nothing about it? Now then, let me advise you how you can save your own life and the life of your son Solomon. Go in to King David and say to him, 'My lord the king, did you not swear to me your servant: "Surely Solomon your son shall be king after me, and he will sit on my throne"? Why then has Adonijah become king?' While you are still there talking to the king, I will come in and add my word to what you have said." (1 Kings 1:11-14)

Nathan's and Bathsheba's lives were potentially on the line. A change in leadership would mean changes for everyone, those who stayed in power and those who would be eliminated as threats.

The Bible doesn't tell us if David actually made that vow, or if he did, why. It might have been a promise born of David's guilt because of the way he had wronged Bathsheba in murdering her husband, and because he felt responsible for the death of their first son. Or it might have been because David had come to truly love Bathsheba, and he wanted the child of his love to sit on his throne. As with the stories of Isaac and Joseph, we see the younger son raised up in the story of God.

In any case, Bathsheba and Nathan had a game plan.

Bathsheba went to see the aged king in his room, where Abishag the Shunammite was attending him. Bathsheba bowed down, prostrating herself before the king.

"What is it you want?" the king asked.

She said to him, "My lord, you yourself swore to me your servant by the LORD your God: 'Solomon your son shall be king after me, and he will sit on my throne.' But now Adonijah has become king, and you, my lord the king, do not know about it. He has sacrificed great numbers of cattle, fattened calves, and sheep, and has invited all the king's sons, Abiathar the priest and Joab the commander of the army, but he has not invited Solomon your servant. My lord the king, the eyes of all Israel are on you, to learn from you who will sit on the throne of my lord the king after him. Otherwise, as soon as my lord the king is laid to rest with his ancestors, I and my son Solomon will be treated as criminals." (1 Kings 1:15–21)

Reading this, it's hard not to think, *Wow! Where was this woman earlier?* Bathsheba went from saying nothing at all to speaking boldly in entire paragraphs! Over the years, it seems, Bathsheba had become an eloquent, fearless woman who was canny enough to know what was going on in the city and brave enough to advocate for her son, Solomon. She was smart in the way she approached the king. She hit David where he was most vulnerable—his pride. She told him that Adonijah was behaving as king, "and you, my lord the king, do not know about it." And then she showed him a way to gain his pride and his honor back, reminding him that "the eyes of all Israel are on you." Perhaps she was appealing to his past, when he was the center of attention, a glamorous young war captain cheered by the women of Jerusalem. But she also knew David's awareness that his voice still carried weight in Israel. Bathsheba knew very well what she was doing, and exactly which buttons to push.

What could this change in Bathsheba mean? For one thing, of course, she was older and surer of herself. But if she was largely silent before, it was because she had only herself to advocate for. Now, she was a mother, and in defense of her son Solomon she had become fearless. How ironic that Bathsheba made an alliance with the very man who confronted David about his shameful sin in taking Bathsheba and having her husband killed. It's clear she had a fondness for him, having named one of her other sons Nathan!

Right on cue, Nathan showed up and repeated the story: Adonijah was declaring himself king, celebrating lavishly and putting together his new administration while David was on his deathbed. David jumped into action before it was too late, saying before Bathsheba:

The king then took an oath: "As surely as the LORD lives, who has delivered me out of every trouble, I will surely carry out this very day what I swore to you by the LORD, the God of Israel: Solomon your son shall be king after me, and he will sit on my throne in my place." (1 Kings 1:29-30)

And to make it official, David called in some of his most trusted men, including Nathan.

> He said to them: "Take your lord's servants with you and have Solomon my son mount my own mule and take him down to Gihon. There have Zadok the priest and Nathan the prophet anoint him king over Israel. Blow the trumpet and shout, 'Long live King Solomon!' Then you are to go up with him, and he is to come and sit on my throne and reign in my place. I have appointed him ruler over Israel and Judah." (1 Kings 1:33–35)

David left no room for discussion, and Solomon became king. It was the worst possible news for the feasting Adonijah and his guests.

> At this, all Adonijah's guests rose in alarm and dispersed. But Adonijah, in fear of Solomon, went and took hold of the horns of the altar. (1 Kings 1:49–50)

The game was over, and Adonijah—and anyone allied with him—was now in real trouble. Going to cling to the horns of the altar in the tabernacle was basically a last-ditch effort at not being killed, a place of safety. And so the negotiations began.

> Then Solomon was told, "Adonijah is afraid of King Solomon and is clinging to the horns of the altar. He says, 'Let King Solomon swear to me today that he will not put his servant to death with the sword.'"
>
> Solomon replied, "If he shows himself to be worthy,

not a hair of his head will fall to the ground; but if evil is found in him, he will die." (1 Kings 1:51-52)

With a deal in place to spare his life, Adonijah was permitted to return home safely. But he would soon reveal himself to be less than wise.

After David's death, as Solomon was busy cementing his hold on the throne, something fascinating happened: Bathsheba was petitioned by Adonijah himself.

Now Adonijah, the son of Haggith, went to Bathsheba, Solomon's mother. Bathsheba asked him, "Do you come peacefully?"

He answered, "Yes, peacefully." Then he added, "I have something to say to you."

"You may say it," she replied.

"As you know," he said, "the kingdom was mine. All Israel looked to me as their king. But things changed, and the kingdom has gone to my brother; for it has come to him from the LORD. Now I have one request to make of you. Do not refuse me."

"You may make it," she said. So he continued, "Please ask King Solomon—he will not refuse you—to give me Abishag the Shunammite as my wife."

"Very well," Bathsheba replied, "I will speak to the king for you." (1 Kings 2:13-18)

This may seem like an odd, but relatively unobtrusive, request to us. David had not slept with this young woman. But remember, she was considered part of David's kingdom, his kingdom.

In those days, taking possession of someone's harem or wives was seen as a power grab. Adonijah knew he couldn't approach King Solomon with a request like that. Adonijah's (not-very-smart) plan meant that he would need someone the king trusted to be his advocate—and whom did Solomon trust more than his mother? Bathsheba had become not just the mother of the king but also his most trusted counselor. If you wanted something done, the implication is, you had to go through her. She probably had a line of people waiting at her door every morning, hoping to persuade her to take their petitions to the king. Bathsheba had clearly become a force to be reckoned with in the kingdom.

What could account for this change? The idea that the mother of the king exercised special prerogatives appears nowhere in the Bible before Bathsheba. In fact, the name of King David's mother never even appears in the Bible at all! Adonijah and Absalom are mentioned as being the sons of David's wife Haggith, but she never makes an appearance in the story either. So Bathsheba's prominence has but one explanation: her son Solomon.

For reasons we can only speculate about, the bond between Bathsheba and Solomon must have been an extraordinary one. Look at how King Solomon greeted his mother when she entered his presence:

When Bathsheba went to King Solomon to speak to him for Adonijah, the king stood up to meet her, bowed down to her and sat down on his throne. He had a throne brought for the king's mother, and she sat down at his right hand.

"I have one small request to make of you," she said. "Do not refuse me."

The king replied, "Make it, my mother; I will not refuse you." (1 Kings 2:19–20)

Solomon immediately saw Adonijah's bid to marry Abishag as just more rebellious plotting on his brother's part. Though Scripture doesn't tell us, I often wonder whether Bathsheba *knew* that's exactly how Adonijah's appeal would come across to Solomon—making her happy to deliver the inappropriate request. And even though Solomon wouldn't fulfill his mother's request, he had no anger toward her. Look at how he had treated Bathsheba upon her arrival. He had a throne brought in just for her, and she sat at his right hand: the place of honor, reserved for the king's chief counselor. This position of the honored queen mother was new. After all, the first two kings of Israel, Saul and David, had come from obscurity, with unheralded parents. But it seems Bathsheba's entire adult life had taken place in the world of palaces and kings. Despite her difficult start, she had finally received a throne of her own.

This is the love of a son for a mother whose devotion to him he has seen over and over again, throughout the years. Were Bathsheba and the beloved Solomon treated as outsiders in the court of King David? Were they the targets of resentment? She may have felt like a cloud covered the bond between her and David, even before David's full treachery came to light, and to have a son to pour her love into after such grief and loss must have been healing for her. It appears Bathsheba and Solomon's bond may have elevated the mothers of kings to a new place of prominence. If you follow the rest of the book of Kings and its long lists of the rulers of Judah, the introduction of each king follows a certain formula. Take a look at Solomon's son Rehoboam:

Rehoboam son of Solomon was king in Judah. He was forty-one years old when he became king, and he reigned seventeen years in Jerusalem, the city the LORD had chosen out of all the tribes of Israel in which to put his Name. *His mother's name was Naamah; she was an Ammonite.* (1 Kings 14:21) [emphasis added]

And look at Rehoboam's son Abijah:

In the eighteenth year of the reign of Jeroboam son of Nebat, Abijah became king of Judah, and he reigned in Jerusalem three years. *His mother's name was Maakah daughter of Abishalom.* (1 Kings 15:1-2) [emphasis added]

It goes on like that, all through both books of Kings, right down to the very last king of Judah, hundreds of years later:

Zedekiah was twenty-one years old when he became king, and he reigned in Jerusalem eleven years. *His mother's name was Hamutal daughter of Jeremiah; she was from Libnah.* (2 Kings 24:18) [emphasis added]

From that point on, in every single introduction of a king of Judah, the mother's name is mentioned alongside the king's. In fact, the term *queen* in the records of the kings of Judah means not the king's wife, but the king's mother! Such was the honor paid by Solomon to his mother that the tradition of the queen mother was forever ingrained in the story of Israel.

Sometimes as a mother you may think that all your devotion to your children—all the countless hours spent making lunches or driving to doctors' appointments and sports practices or organizing meals and vacation and laundry—has gone unnoticed. The kids pile out of the car without a backward glance or a thank-you, and it can seem like none of it matters. Bathsheba probably had those days with Solomon, but it's clear her son treasured her counsel and care. If you are a mother, you are constantly planting seeds of love and guidance—though you may sometimes wonder if you'll see the fruit of that this side of heaven.

For Bathsheba, who walked through devastating loss in the death of her first son, part of her reward was the joy of seeing Solomon seated on the throne, which was largely the result of her willingness to speak up and intervene with the help of Nathan. What might have happened to Israel under Adonijah's rule? Instead, the nation was led by a man often called the wisest to ever live.

In 1 Kings 3, we see the Lord was pleased and said to Solomon, "Ask for whatever you want me to give you" (1 Kings 3:5). Here's how their conversation went:

> "So give your servant a discerning heart to govern your people and to distinguish between right and wrong. For who is able to govern this great people of yours?"
> The LORD was pleased that Solomon had asked for this. So God said to him, "Since you have asked for this and not for long life or wealth for yourself, nor have asked for the death of your enemies but for discernment in administering justice, I will do what you have asked. I will give you a wise and discerning heart, so that there will never have been anyone like you, nor will there ever be. Moreover, I will give you what you have not asked for—both wealth

and honor—so that in your lifetime you will have no equal among kings. (1 Kings 3:9-13)

Amazing on so many levels! A man humble enough to know he needed what only God could give him: the wisdom to guide the people under his care. And a God generous enough to give him not only that, but wealth and honor to boot!

Bathsheba, a woman so often disregarded (then and now) and one who endured excruciating loss, gave birth to the man who would bless God's people abundantly through his wisdom and kind rule. Not only that, but she was instrumental in making sure Solomon found his way to the throne. There is so much more to Bathsheba's story than you may have known, and the Bible is full of other compelling people who may have been quite different from what you thought! They are complex and flawed *and* used by God, which is reassuring and welcome news for all of us.

Lord God, Sustainer in our grief and in our joy: give us the strength to bring our heartbreak to you. Transform our grief with the power of Your presence. Give us the courage to face suffering and sorrow and loss. Please remind our fragile hearts that You are always working for the greater good of Your ultimate plans, which are for Your glory. Help us to know that our beginnings and circumstances do not dictate our joy and that the seeds of our pain and past may give bloom to bountiful, beautiful fruit beyond our imaginations.

Bathsheba Study Questions

1. What was your impression of Bathsheba before reading this chapter? Did your perception of her change after studying her story? If so, how? Why do you think she is sometimes portrayed in a way that doesn't line up with Scripture?

2. What were the numerous decisions by David that resulted in Bathsheba's pregnancy? Were there warning signs and opportunities for him to put the brakes on his attraction to her? (2 Samuel 11:2–4)

3. After learning Bathsheba was pregnant with his child, how did David actively choose to dig even deeper into his pattern of sin? (2 Samuel 11:6–26) Did David express remorse over his decisions? Have you ever entered into a season of willful sin? What lies did the enemy tell you about what you were doing?

4. How did David react when confronted with his sin? What does true repentance look like? (2 Samuel 12:1–23) What does God promise to those who confess their sins, repent, and turn from them? (Psalm 103:12; 1 John 1:9)

5. What do we learn about David's parenting style, and how did that impact the behavior of his sons?

6. How did Solomon ultimately become king? What was Bathsheba's role? What do we know about the kind of man she had raised in Solomon? (1 Kings 3:7–14) Contrast Bathsheba's role as a mother with Rebekah's. What can we glean about their mothering in light of how their sons turned out?

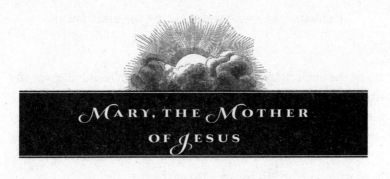

MARY, THE MOTHER OF JESUS

(Luke 1, Luke 2:22–35, Matthew 2:13–18,
Luke 2:41–52, John 2:1–11, John 19:22–27, Acts 1:12–14)

When we think of biblical motherhood, we often think of Mary first. From the beginning, she is offered to us as an example of deep faith and trust in a situation that was unlike any other. Profoundly humbled by her assignment as the earthly vessel for the Savior, she rejoiced in her calling—even though she had to know many would never understand or believe the story. Mary's joy as a mother must have been immense: the elation of receiving the angel Gabriel's message that she was chosen to be the mother of the Messiah, the pride she must have felt in watching her divine son grow up and begin His ministry, the euphoria she experienced at His Resurrection. But hers was a story also marked by deep grief and sacrifice.

We most often focus on Mary around Christmastime each year, as the radiant young mother overwhelmed by the miracle happening in her own body. We contemplate the tenderness and wonder with which she must have held her newborn son, God in the flesh. When we happen upon a Christmas crèche or nativity scene, we consider the peace and joy that seem to radiate from her sweet face, as everything is bathed in a golden Christmas glow. But this is just the beginning of Mary's life as a mother. Along the way she would experience grief only a mother who has lost a child can understand, and before that ever happened, she would watch as her son was mocked, falsely accused, and rejected by the very people He was trying to save. As great as Mary's joy was at her son's birth, her sorrow later in His life was just as intense.

Motherhood is like that too, sometimes—a confusing mix of emotions. There can be celebration, anxiety, exhaustion, bliss, and depression. Mothers can worry about their children, be perplexed by them, and be blessed by them—all in the same day! As children grow into their own independence, mothers can wonder what happened to the closeness they once shared. There are times when motherhood itself may feel like more of a burden than a joy—the endless (and frequently thankless) work of it, the exhaustion, the laundry and the cooking and the countless questions, the micromanagement of running a household with small (and bigger!) children in it. Our faith doesn't require mothers to pretend that they don't feel overwhelmed at times. Motherhood will always be a mix of the highest highs and lowest lows, a reflection of our broader life in this fallen world. There is no Easter without Calvary, and every mother's journey will be marked by both delight and despair. So let us walk along on Mary's path, discovering ways to navigate both.

SIMEON'S PROPHECY

At the end of the nativity narrative in the Gospel of Luke, we see Mary and Joseph arriving at the temple in Jerusalem to present their son to the Lord forty days after His birth, according to the customs of Jewish law. A sacrifice was offered, prayers were made, and the whole experience must have been a beautiful and exciting one for the parents. Mary must have been so proud, walking into those hallowed temple precincts holding her infant son close, knowing in her heart of hearts that she was cradling in her arms the temple's Lord. Mary and Joseph also experienced the joy of seeing other people—the holy Simeon and the righteous Anna—who recognized their son for who He was.

Simeon held the baby Jesus in his arms and prayed these famous words, thanking God for allowing him to live to see the day of the Messiah's arrival:

> Sovereign LORD, as you have promised,
>   you may now dismiss your servant in peace.
>   For my eyes have seen your salvation,
>   which you have prepared in the sight of all nations:
>   a light for revelation to the Gentiles,
>   and the glory of your people Israel. (Luke 2:29-32)

This poetic Song of Simeon (known as the *Nunc Dimittis*, from the opening lines in Latin, "Now let depart") became a central part of evening prayers for ancient and medieval Christians, when they would pray that God would "dismiss" them into the rest of sleep. This song is a glorious acknowledgment of the fullness of God's revelation in Christ, and it must have made Mary's heart swell with joy to hear her precious baby recognized as the salvation not just of Israel but of "all nations" (Luke 2:31).

But Simeon wasn't finished with his prophecy just yet. He had more to say, specifically to Mary:

> The child's father and mother marveled at what was said about him. Then Simeon blessed them and said to Mary,

his mother: "This child is destined to cause the falling and rising of many in Israel, and to be a sign that will be spoken against, so that the thoughts of many hearts will be revealed. And a sword will pierce your own soul too." (Luke 2:33–35)

These mysterious words would have been harder to hear and understand than Simeon's previous promises of light and peace. In this prophecy, Jesus would cause not just the rise but also the fall of many. Simeon went on to call the baby "a sign that will be spoken against" (Luke 2:34). The road for Mary's little boy would not be an easy one, and Simeon was the first one to give this young mother that difficult news: an annunciation of a different sort. People would speak out against Jesus, they would argue about Him, and they would say things about Him that would reveal their own darkest thoughts. And as if all that were not enough, Simeon told Mary that the pain that lay ahead was not just for Jesus but also for her. "A sword will pierce your own soul too," he said to her (Luke 2:35). That's not exactly the sort of thing you want written on a baby shower cake!

The hard fact is, Simeon was telling the truth not just about the painful events that were on the horizon for Mary's life but also about Christian discipleship. If you remember the day and the hour in which you surrendered your life to Christ as His own forever, you recall it as one of incredible joy and freedom. And it was! But it was also something more: that day was your first step on a challenging road. All of us who follow Christ must walk His path, and He made clear it wouldn't be all mountaintops.

Then Jesus said to his disciples, "Whoever wants to be my disciple must deny themselves and take up their cross and follow me. For whoever wants to save their life will lose it, but whoever loses their life for me will find it." (Matthew 16:24–25)

The Christian walk requires commitment and humility, and the words of Simeon are important for us all to ponder, not just Mary. Did she ever want to turn back? Did she want to say to God, "Never mind; it's too hard. The angel didn't tell me about this part"?

We never see Mary trying to back out of her divine assignment. Not once in her conversation with Gabriel had she said, "Wait, tell me what's going to happen to me." She simply asked the angel *how* it was going to happen, and then she said, "I am the LORD's servant" (Luke 1:38). However, this doesn't mean that she knew immediately just how difficult Jesus's path would be. Mary's famous Magnificat prayer in Luke 1:46-55 ended on a note of praise, thanking God for remembering Israel. Here in the temple, forty days after Jesus's birth, may have marked the first time it truly occurred to Mary that the ending of her son's story might not be the one for which she had been hoping and praying.

MARY THE REFUGEE

Mothers want only the best for their children. So much of the time leading up to their arrival is about nesting. Family and friends usually come together to help provide the basics you need to create a safe environment that's warm and welcoming. Everyone wants a nursery space for their little one, with a sturdy crib and soft sheets and blankets—maybe some wall art or matching curtains. There is great delight in crafting a beautiful physical place for that baby to begin growing and in dreaming of all the firsts to come. The last thing any mother wants is to have to snatch up her baby and run for her life, but that is exactly what Mary had to do.

A dire warning and clear directive came straight from heaven right after the Magi left. Though these wise men from the East had previously promised to tell King Herod the whereabouts of the new Messiah, they were warned in a dream not to return to Herod. Instead, they traveled home via a different route. Meanwhile, an angel appeared to Joseph and instructed him to flee to Egypt to escape Herod's evil plan.

> When they had gone, an angel of the LORD appeared to Joseph in a dream. "Get up," he said, "take the child and his mother and escape to Egypt. Stay there until I tell you, for Herod is going to search for the child to kill him."
>
> So he got up, took the child and his mother during the night and left for Egypt, where he stayed until the death of Herod. And so was fulfilled what the LORD had said through the prophet: "Out of Egypt I called my son." (Matthew 2:13–15)

In essence, Joseph was living out parallels to his namesake—a chosen man who was gifted with the ability to understand important dreams—and one whose journey to save the nation of Israel led him through Egypt. I wonder if Jesus's devout human parents took note of the similarities.

They were faithful to God's guidance, and Herod was not happy about it.

When Herod realized that he had been outwitted by the Magi, he was furious, and he gave orders to kill all the boys in Bethlehem and its vicinity who were two years old and under, in accordance with the time he had learned from the Magi. Then what was said through the prophet Jeremiah was fulfilled:

"A voice is heard in Ramah,
weeping and great mourning,
Rachel weeping for her children
and refusing to be comforted,
because they are no more." (Matthew 2:16–18)

Herod's murderous rage would not stop until he believed Jesus had been wiped off the face of the earth. Joseph and Mary had no choice but to run as far away as possible, somewhere Herod would have no authority to hurt them even if he was able to track them down. They ran to the Roman province of Egypt. Unlike Judea, which had kept its system of native kingship in place alongside the Roman administration, Egypt was under the direct rule of the Roman emperor himself. Herod would have found it much harder to persuade Roman officials there to do his bidding. There was no one he could order around in Egypt. Besides, in the bustling metropolises of Egypt and among the thriving Jewish communities there, an obscure couple and their child would be nearly impossible to find. They were safe there, but at what cost?

The journey would have been long and exhausting. The young family, probably leaving their native land for the first time, set out across the rugged plains of Sinai carrying a toddler, trudging through thirst and weariness across an expanse of sand and rugged hills. Finally, they emerged in the greenery of the Nile delta, glowing in contrast to the surrounding sands. The Sphinx, then with face undamaged, would have been an astounding sight. The battered trio likely gazed in awe at the already ancient Pyramids, including the Great Pyramid, one of what we know now as the Seven Wonders of the World. It must have been overwhelming.

These grand new sights unfolded at the end of a journey sparked by that harrowing moment when Joseph awoke and knew they had to flee. By the way, the Scripture tells us that Joseph didn't hesitate, but "took the child and his mother during the night and left for Egypt" (Matthew 2:14). Notice that they left "during the night." For Mary, it must have been hectic and terrifying, to be roused—not to tend to her frightened or hungry child—but by her husband, speaking insistently about a dream he was given by God. Mary was a woman who'd heard from God before, and in her faith, there was no hesitation to get moving. Mary and Joseph slipped out of Bethlehem in the darkness, Mary holding Jesus close. Was this mother praying her precious son would stay quiet as they tried to put as many miles as possible between themselves and Herod's assassins?

But in addition to being afraid, Mary may also have been tempted to despair. After all, this probably wasn't how she thought her story was going to go! Her son was supposed to be the Messiah who would save His people, the great glory of Israel. And now they were fleeing in the night, running away from the land of Israel—forever, it could be. They would have had no idea when (or even if) they would ever be able to return. Without much chance to say good-bye to family and friends, without more than a few hastily gathered belongings, they were leaving their old life behind and setting out for a new one. Simeon's prophecy seemed to be coming true, long before she had even thought it might.

Was Mary doubting herself as a mother, the earthly mother of the Son of God? The Lord of the whole universe had entrusted her with His only Son, and she wasn't able to provide Him a permanent place to call home. The young Messiah was less than two years old, and He was already on the run. The kind of life that she probably expected to give Him—that she had wanted so desperately to provide for Him—seemed to be an impossibility now.

Any mother who has ever faced financial difficulty knows something of the pain Mary, a homeless refugee, felt on that journey to Egypt. It's easier to do without for ourselves, but it's a much more painful scenario when it comes to our children. I have no doubt my mother struggled financially during the years it was just the two of us. I remember our clunker of a car regularly breaking down and lots of baloney and ketchup sandwiches, but we had each other and plenty of laughter too. My mom was an expert at shielding me from the realities of our situation, and my grandparents were always present to help and care for us when we needed it most. I look back now and wonder how a single mother in her mid-twenties managed to work nonstop, sew our clothes, and make me believe my childhood was magical! My mother-in-law, Jouetta, together with her husband, raised six kids on a tight budget and did the same thing. In both my and my husband's family, our mothers modeled faith, perseverance, and grit. Mary would have needed those in abundant supply.

Mothers have real anxieties about their children's futures when it comes to things like choosing a college or enlisting in the military. Will they choose friends whose influence will be positive, or will they get tangled up with people who draw them into addiction or danger? Who will they marry, and when can we expect grandkids? But let's take that one step further. What about mothers who truly don't know where their next meal is coming from? What about the mother who flees the chaos of a collapsing country or the poverty or violence that threatens her child's life? She is journeying on a path that Mary and Jesus knew.

We walk the path of Mary too when our plans for our children turn out very differently from what we had imagined. Just as Mary held Christ close on that perilous journey to Egypt, we too must cling to Christ through our most daunting seasons. Because we know the end of Mary's story, it's easy for us to see that what may have felt like failure, fear, and despair to Mary was just the beginning of a far larger and more glorious adventure. When you see your children suffering, it's often hard to take the long view of your own story. Scripture reminds us, however, that God is ever present. He is as interested in the details of your struggle as He was in the plight of Mary and Joseph all those centuries ago. That family on the run finally arrived to witness the pomp and glory of Egypt. Yet, for all the glitz and glamor of those human achievements, Mary knew that the child she was carrying in her arms was a greater wonder than all of them.

JESUS IN THE TEMPLE

After Herod's death, an angel of the Lord once again appeared to Joseph in a dream, telling him it was safe to return to Israel. This time, Jesus and His parents hiked all the way north to Nazareth, which became His home. Luke closes his early narrative with an interesting story, one in which Jesus speaks for the first time:

Every year Jesus's parents went to Jerusalem for the Festival of the Passover. When he was twelve years old, they went up to the festival, according to the custom. After the festival was over, while his parents were returning home, the boy Jesus stayed behind in Jerusalem, but they were unaware of it. Thinking he was in their company, they traveled on for a day. Then they began looking for him among their relatives and friends. When they did not find him, they went back to Jerusalem to look for him. After three days they found him in the temple courts, sitting among the teachers, listening to them and asking them questions. Everyone who heard him was amazed at his understanding and his answers. (Luke 2:41–47)

This story is often used to highlight the beginnings of Christ's mission on earth. We see someone wise beyond His years, unafraid to be alone and on His own in a big city, fully engaged with the religious teachers at the temple. If you've heard the story, *especially* if you've heard it many times, that may be where you initially focus. But let's not forget—at the heart of this passage—there was a frantic mother whose son had been missing for days!

When his parents saw him, they were astonished. His mother said to him, "Son, why have you treated us like this? Your father and I have been anxiously searching for you." (Luke 2:48)

Mary must have been enormously relieved to lay eyes on her son, knowing he was safe and unharmed. Yes, she knew He had a divine destiny, but it seems she hadn't anticipated He would be so young when it started to reveal itself. She was clearly taken aback, *How could you let us fear and panic like this?!*

In the previous two passages we looked at in this chapter—the prophecy of Simeon, and the flight into Egypt—Mary suffered as a mother because of outside forces. She experienced foreboding at the words of Simeon, and she experienced fear at the prospect of Herod's assassins. But in this grief, it was Jesus Himself who was the source of her pain. Can you imagine what those three days must have been like for Mary? Even one hour of not knowing where your children are and being unable to protect them, where they might be lost and confused and crying out for you, is agony. It is a grief that hundreds of thousands of mothers experience every year. Hundreds of thousands of children in the United States go missing every year, leaving mothers worried and desperate, swinging between hope and despair until that child is located. For a few unbearable days, Mary was one of those mothers. But she lived in a world where mothers had no access to call up 9-1-1 and rally police to help in the search. She lived in a time without cell phones, no social media where she could post her son's picture, lacking a way to quickly stay in contact with any leads from friends and family who also must have been searching.

In the midst of this story, it is easy to miss a telling detail—the number of days: "after three days they found him in the temple courts" (Luke 2:46). Jesus was missing from his distraught parents for three days, just as He would later be absent from His grieving followers for three long days. On the third day, Mary had a foreshadowing of the joy of the Resurrection to come when she finally caught sight of her son. And He was whole, well, and alive! As much as she must have been grateful for what seemed like a miracle, Mary asked the same question any mother in that situation would have asked: "Why have you treated us like this?" Jesus responded:

> "Why were you searching for me?" he asked. "Didn't you know I had to be in my Father's house?" But they did not understand what he was saying to them. (Luke 2:49–50)

Was Jesus's reply a cold splash of water to Mary's face? *Why were you even looking for me?* Mama of the Savior of the world or not, I'm guessing that hit Mary right in the heart. Interestingly, Jesus did not really answer the question. (Admittedly, many of us can relate to a twelve-year-old evading a direct question!) Jesus acted instead as if it was the most natural thing in the world for Him to be exactly where He was, in the temple. Some translations say that Jesus asked His parents, "Did you not know that I must be about My Father's business?" (Luke 2:49 NKJV), as if their worry made no sense. Mary and Joseph knew their oldest son was unmistakably divine, the Son of God, but had they lost sight of His heavenly mission in the midst of raising and family and the busyness of life? Jesus's response must have seemed infuriatingly unsympathetic to His confused parents. The Bible tells us they didn't understand it.

In this passage in Luke 2 we see Mary echoing the feelings of her ancestors who also found themselves bewildered by God's mysterious plans at times. Rebekah, Rachel, Jochebed—these women must have felt like God's plans went off the rails when their sons were thrown into exile. In fact, these unexpected twists were key parts of God's final plan. While Mary had a warning in the form of Simeon's prophecy about Jesus's chaotic future, she still couldn't fully see the ultimate shape of God's plan. Jesus's disappearance must have first frightened her, and then it probably confused her as she found Him safe and unaware of the panic His absence had caused. It must have been puzzling at times to consider His divine nature as He grew from child to adolescent to adult. Scripture tells us their family returned to normal—though it was certainly a *new* normal—after this unsettling incident in Jerusalem.

> **Then he went down to Nazareth with them and was obedient to them. But his mother treasured all these things in her heart. And Jesus grew in wisdom and stature, and in favor with God and man. (Luke 2:51-52)**

This story in Luke is the first, last, and only glimpse we have of Jesus's childhood. After this, all the Gospel narratives transition quickly to Jesus as an adult. The story of Mary's suffering is more familiar to us from this point on. We can more easily imagine the grief she must have known as the mother of a falsely-accused, executed man. For mothers who suffer as they watch their grown children struggle to find their way and choose things that we know will bring them pain, Mary has walked your path too. The mother of Jesus lived all those things. Jesus was on a mission to sacrifice in a way that certainly caused those closest to him enormous grief, but with the larger goal of providing a means of salvation for every single one of us. Mary was blessed among women, but was also asked as a mother to continually surrender her son and to watch as He was misunderstood and abused. What grace and maturity she modeled for us as she "treasured" all those realities in her human heart.

MARY AT CANA

The Gospel of John gives us our only glimpse of an interaction between the adult Jesus and His mother that is not connected to the final days of His life. At a wedding in Cana, Mary urged Jesus to begin His public ministry. Some scholars believe Mary may have been connected to the wedding party through family ties or friendship, which is why she felt some level of responsibility for the enjoyment of the guests at the reception. Assuming Mary had truly come to terms with the fact that Jesus's road ahead would be a challenging one, it would have taken true selflessness to tell her son, "This is the time. Don't wait any longer." But it's also not clear whether Mary, lovingly and totally confident in her divine firstborn, knew what she was asking when she brought this minor domestic problem to His attention.

On the third day a wedding took place at Cana in Galilee. Jesus' mother was there, and Jesus and his disciples had also been invited to the wedding. When the wine was gone, Jesus' mother said to him, "They have no more wine."

"Woman, why do you involve me?" Jesus replied. "My hour has not yet come."

His mother said to the servants, "Do whatever he tells you." (John 2:1–5)

On the surface of it, what an odd place to begin a ministry of miracles and preaching! Our earthly minds may think a Sabbath morning in the local synagogue would have been more appropriate. Maybe Jesus's first miracle should have been a truly dramatic event: an exorcism, a raising from the dead, a healing that no one could have expected. But that wasn't what happened. Jesus's first miracle was performed at a small wedding celebration among family and friends. The ministry that would take Him to the cross began in joy, in the midst of human rejoicing—a wedding that was perhaps a foreshadowing of the wedding of Christ to the church, still to come. And in the middle of all that celebrating, there was an embarrassing reminder of the hosts' limitations: no more wine.

Notice that Mary did not go to Jesus and say, "What do You think about this?" or, "Maybe You should think about helping them out." All she did was present Him with the information and leave Him to make His own choice. Jesus spoke colloquially and informally to His mother, in words that are difficult to translate into English. What He literally said is, "What to me and to you, woman? Not yet has come the hour of me." My initial reading of this story years ago was that Jesus sounded rather brusque. However, digging into the original language helps us to see that wasn't the case at all. Simply addressing Mary as "woman" may sound a bit disrespectful or abrupt in English, but let's look at the Greek. In the original language, it is a polite and respectful term—something like "ma'am" or "dear lady" in English. It was formal, but firm; Jesus let Mary know He alone would respond as He deemed appropriate.

John the Baptist says of Jesus later in the Gospel of John, "He must become greater, and I must become less" (John 3:30). Every mother knows this moment, of learning when to step back and let your child take the lead. It will happen again and again as a child becomes an adult, spreading his or her wings of independence. Mary serves as our example here, deferring to God's ultimate purposes and plans. At that wedding, Jesus did begin revealing His divine nature, setting into motion more than His own mother could ever have imagined would come.

> Nearby stood six stone water jars, the kind used by the Jews for ceremonial washing, each holding from twenty to thirty gallons.
>
> Jesus said to the servants, "Fill the jars with water"; so they filled them to the brim.
>
> Then he told them, "Now draw some out and take it to the master of the banquet."
>
> They did so, and the master of the banquet tasted the water that had been turned into wine. He did not realize where it had come from, though the servants who had drawn the water knew. Then he called the bridegroom aside and said, "Everyone brings out the choice wine first and then the cheaper wine after the guests have had too much to drink; but you have saved the best till now."
>
> What Jesus did here in Cana of Galilee was the first of the signs through which he revealed his glory; and his disciples believed in him. (John 2:6–11)

Notice that last line. Mary already knew what it appears the disciples discovered and embraced in a real way that day: Jesus's truly divine nature. These men had been following Jesus, listening to His teachings without yet having seen a miracle. Now they had, and the journey was underway.

MARY, MOTHER OF GRIEF

We cannot forget that, though Jesus was Mary's oldest, He was not her only child. We know of at least the named siblings James,

Joseph, Simon, and Judas (Jude)—and unnamed sisters too (Matthew 6:3, 13:55-56; Mark 6:3). Mary had undoubtedly been busy raising her growing family while also remembering the promises and prophecies regarding her firstborn son. Despite the many responsibilities she must have had, in Jesus's final days Mary was not far away. Was she there as the crowds jubilantly cheered Jesus on His entry into Jerusalem?

> And the crowds that went before him and that followed him were shouting, "Hosanna to the Son of David! Blessed is he who comes in the name of the LORD! Hosanna in the highest!" (Matthew 21:9)

> And those who went before and those who followed were shouting, "Hosanna! Blessed is he who comes in the name of the LORD! Blessed is the coming kingdom of our father David! Hosanna in the highest!" (Mark 11:9-10)

> As he was drawing near—already on the way down the Mount of Olives—the whole multitude of his disciples began to rejoice and praise God with a loud voice for all the mighty works that they had seen, saying, "Blessed is the King who comes in the name of the LORD! Peace in heaven and glory in the highest!" (Luke 19:37-38)

> The next day the large crowd that had come to the feast heard that Jesus was coming to Jerusalem. So they took branches of palm trees and went out to meet him, crying out, "Hosanna! Blessed is he who comes in the name of the LORD, even the King of Israel!" (John 12:12-13)

Imagine being a witness to this kind of rapturous reception and praise for your own son. From long before He was born into human form, Mary knew exactly who Jesus was, "the Son of the Most High." She had heard the prophecy that He would sit on the throne of His "father David. . . . his kingdom will never end" (Luke 1:32–33). She had also seen the criticism and attacks of those who did not believe. As Jesus entered Jerusalem, I wonder if there was some part of Mary that thought, *Now they get it. They finally see and accept Jesus as their Messiah and Savior.* Or were the words of Simeon—promising not just salvation but also suffering—still tucked into her memory bank, a warning of what was still to come?

Mary was likely a witness to everything that happened to Jesus that week. Since she is mentioned at the cross, Mary likely would have been with the disciples in Jerusalem, traveling with them to support and help however she could. Because of the quick, sham trial of Jesus and the almost immediate crucifixion, Mary would not have had time to travel the many miles from Nazareth to Jerusalem on such short notice. We can assume that Mary was part of the inner circle who traveled with Jesus in his last months and weeks—and probably from before then.

During that time of traveling with Jesus, did Mary ever think that the road might end on a Roman cross? As a woman who grew up in occupied Roman territory, she may have. Crucifixion would not have been a new sight to her. The brutality of the Roman state was a part of her everyday life. That her own people's religious authorities would collude with the Roman state to bring about Jesus's execution—that was a plot twist she would not have foreseen. But she would have seen the anger of the men who argued with Him—the ones He consistently silenced with His knowledge and truth. She had likely heard the threats against Jesus.

How quickly the cheering crowds of Jerusalem morphed into holding a phony trial, which led to torture and a death sentence for Mary's beloved son. The mother of Jesus had to endure the sight of her son leaving those courts bloodied, beaten, and broken. She had to witness His nearly impossible struggle up to the place of His own execution. She had to stand by as her son's flesh and muscles were run through with iron nails. What she may not have anticipated was that Jesus would make no effort to save Himself. She might have thought what His disciples (including Judas) surely thought—that if push came to shove, and Jesus was dragged into a court, Roman or otherwise, He would use His formidable power to free Himself and prove that He was the Messiah.

Jesus's closest disciples had witnessed who He truly was in the weeks preceding His arrest, when He was transfigured before Peter, James, and John and clothed in all His heavenly glory (Matthew 17:1-9). Certainly that power and glory were well known by His mother. Did she also think that Jesus would use His power to extricate Himself if things ever went too far? Perhaps He at least would use His sharp tongue and sharper mind, the mind that had been confounding doctors of the law since He was twelve, to defend Himself.

The last moment we see Mary in the Gospels is at the foot of the cross. In one of the most heartrending scenes in all of Scripture, Jesus in His dying agony shows concern for His mother and what would happen to her after His death.

Near the cross of Jesus stood his mother, his mother's sister, Mary the wife of Clopas, and Mary Magdalene.

> When Jesus saw his mother there, and the disciple whom he loved standing nearby, he said to her, "Woman, here is your son," and to the disciple, "Here is your mother." From that time on, this disciple took her into his home. (John 19:25–27)

Here at the end of her son's life, Mary shows us how to walk the hardest path of all for any: the way of helplessness.

There is no harder thing than to be powerless in the face of a child's suffering. Any mother sitting up at night with a feverish, miserable child knows this pain. Any mother at a hospital bedside watching a beloved child fight for life knows this agony. *What can I do?* we plead with God in our prayers, and sometimes the answer is: *nothing.* What do we do when the path our child is on is no longer one that we can rescue them from? Where do we find the strength to face our own despair?

Mary found hers at the foot of the cross, which is where we find our strength too. Too often in our churches we are uncomfortable with suffering. We might talk about it, but we don't often like to *see* it. Some people wrongly believe that being a committed Christian means being and feeling happy and optimistic all the time. But Christ Himself warned us that's not reality:

> I have told you these things, so that in me you may have peace. In this world you will have trouble. But take heart! I have overcome the world. (John 16:33)

Christ on the cross calls us to a life of suffering: the daily reality we experience as Christians. But He also reminds us to remember how the story ends. The empty tomb is still the source of our unshakable joy. Mary shows us that the path to ultimate redemption and peace is *through* grief, right through the heart of it and out the other side. We can't avoid the cross on our way to the Resurrection.

The same is true of the path of discipleship that goes through motherhood. For those of you who are mothers, it isn't a question of *whether* you will walk through suffering in your motherhood; it's a question of *when*. Mary's sheer elation when she heard Jesus had risen from the dead is beyond our ability to imagine—or maybe not. Every mother who has embraced a child she thought she'd lost forever, when against all odds she holds that child in her arms again, has known what Mary felt that Easter morning. Mary's joy (and ours) does not happen in spite of the cross; it happens *because* of the cross.

Mary in the Early Church

Mary's last appearance in the Bible is not in the Gospels but in the book of Acts. Her story does not end with Easter—but like the story of the young Christian community, her story begins anew right there.

Then the apostles returned to Jerusalem from the hill called the Mount of Olives, a Sabbath day's walk from the city. When they arrived, they went upstairs to the room where they were staying. Those present were Peter, John, James and Andrew; Philip and Thomas, Bartholomew and Matthew; James son of Alphaeus and Simon the Zealot, and Judas son of James. They all joined together constantly in prayer, along with the women and Mary the mother of Jesus, and with his brothers. (Acts 1:12–14)

After Jesus ascended into heaven, His disciples stayed put in Jerusalem as He had commanded them—directing them to wait for the gift of the Holy Spirit (Acts 1:4). Once Jesus was physically gone from them, they held all the tighter to their tiny community of believers. And that is where we find Mary, faithfully present and gathered in fellowship with Jesus's disciples. Even after her son (in His physical form) was gone from this earth, Mary devoted herself to her son's community. By joining with them, she continued His work after His ascension. She believed in the mission Jesus had given the early church, even when it was simply a handful of people in a rented room.

This would not have been a challenge for Mary, for she had been a believer in Christ longer than any of them. For Mary, to be among excited and nervous new converts must have felt like the fruition of the hopes and dreams she had held in her heart for so long. How far she had come! Jesus's mother had believed Him for thirty-three years, from the moment an angel told her that her entire life would be thrown into chaos by a miracle child. She'd trusted in His promises as she and Joseph stumbled blearily out of bed one night in Bethlehem and fled Herod's soldiers. She'd believed in Him as she sat holding Him close in a mighty land of foreign gods and great palaces. She'd believed as He'd grown up, a confident and unpredictable boy whose expectations were shaped by a kingdom she could not yet see. Knowing Jesus had triumphed over death and seeing the beginnings of His church sprouting up . . . in this Mary was witnessing the fulfillment of promises that the angel Gabriel and the priest Simeon had given her decades before. Finally, she could see in plain sight the once-hidden plans of God that had felt so mysterious.

Presumably, Mary shared these early stories with the fledgling church and the men who would later record them in the Gospels. Mary gave them courage by sharing her own journey. She knew the path ahead would be a hard one, as the disciples struggled to make disciples of their own. They were embarking on a mission to spread the good news of God in Christ to every corner of their world. But this too is often at the heart of motherhood—the investment of slow and steady work, knowing you may not see the end results. Mary would not live to see the church become everything that it would eventually be in the centuries ahead. She probably died before Christianity had taken much root in her homeland.

Mothers devote themselves to a future that will outlive them, and they do so in the footsteps of Mary, who also worked for a promised expectation. They pray over their pregnant bellies, ask God for help through endless sleepless nights, and hope for a time when their children will embrace all the Lord has planned for their destinies. As a daughter, I'm grateful for both my earthly mother, who did all of these things and more, and the spiritual mothers I've been blessed with throughout my life. Some of them have children of their own; others do not. That never stopped them from generously pouring their time and wisdom into me when I so desperately needed it. And now I've come full circle, answering the questions of young women who are in the generation behind me. Careers, relationships, finances, dreams—these issues and more have been the subject of teary phone calls and frantic texts. I am forever grateful for the "mothers" who answered my cries for help and for the opportunities to do that now for the "daughters" God has brought into my life.

Lord God, grant us the steadfastness of Mary in the face of both extraordinary joy and overwhelming sorrow. Help us to pick up our cross and follow You, right through the heart of grief and into the promise of redemption. Teach us to embrace our own helplessness when we see our children suffer, and give us the strength to surrender them to You just as Mary committed her beloved son to You. Remind us that we can all be mothers to those seeking guidance and help through life's challenges. Guide us to be faithful as Mary was, investing our lives in Your church and the gospel mission.

Mary, the Mother of Jesus Study Questions

1. How does Mary model the broad range of emotions and experiences mothers go through? From the beginning, she shows commitment to obedience and trust. (Luke 1:38) How can we develop the same spiritual characteristics in our lives?

2. What was Mary's reaction to Simeon's prophecy about Jesus's life? How would you react to news like this? (Luke 2:28–33)

3. Does Mary and Joseph's journey as refugees impact how you see those in need around the world? How can we draw inspiration from their willingness to follow God's direction, even when it required a perilous trek?

4. Even though they knew Jesus was the Son of God, Mary and Joseph had other children and a busy, ordinary life. Do you think it was easy at times to forget what His mission truly was? (Luke 2:42–52)

5. What do you make of Mary's role in Jesus's first public miracle? (John 2:1–11) What was the resulting impact on the disciples?

6. What do we learn about deep faithfulness through Mary's appearance not only at the foot of the cross, but also with the gathering of believers after Jesus's death and resurrection?

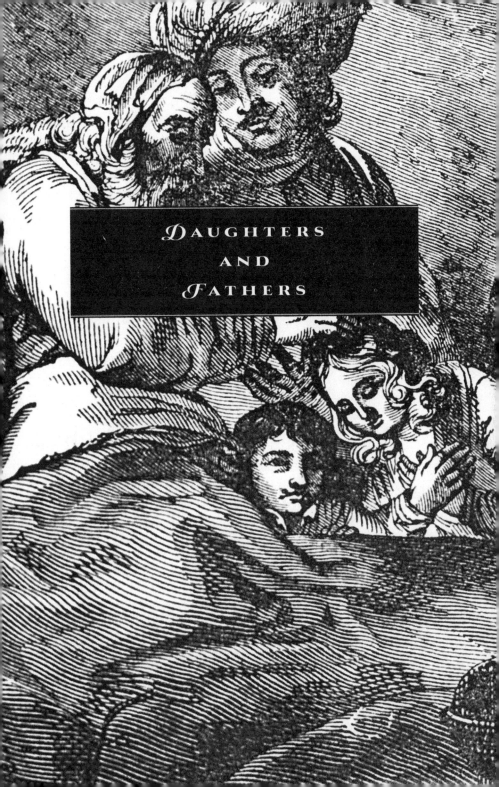

DAUGHTERS
AND
FATHERS

The Bible is full of stories that are uncomfortable and raw, but each is included with a purpose. Often, it's to see the long-term results of disobedience to God's clear commands and directives. Sometimes that shows up in flawed, destructive family relationships. But the stories are never without lessons and hope. By looking at the mistakes made by earthly mothers and fathers, we can even more clearly see the power of God when He redeems them for good.

By examining the stories of these imperfect families we can also gather tools and insights for dealing with our modern-day challenges. God is faithful when we lay our deepest fears and frustrations at His feet. He's waiting to patch back together the wounds on our hearts. He is the Father who will never abandon or reject us. We are precious in His sight, no matter our earthly circumstances.

Father figures can guide us, teaching us obedience and bravery so that we will be able to confront the enemy when he shows up in the details of our daily journey. By equipping and encouraging us, and speaking the truth when we need it most, godly men can prepare us for the path God has mapped for us long before the foundations of the world we know.

DINAH

(Genesis 34)

DINAH THE DAUGHTER OF ISRAEL

Many stories in Genesis are tough to read. But it's important to delve into these parts of the Bible, as difficult as they may be. There are ugly sins to confront and hard truths to digest. If we truly want to understand God's character and His plans, we can't skip over the stories that don't have happy endings. What we can do is learn from devastating mistakes and the consequences of purposeful disobedience and sin. The story of Jacob and Leah's daughter, Dinah, is one of those stories—full of horrible, broken people. One heinous decision piled on top of another until there was almost nothing left but a wasteland of violence and destruction, both emotional and physical.

When the story begins, we learn that Jacob and his family were living just outside the city of Shechem, having purchased land there (Genesis 33:18–20). That would appear to be in conflict with the direction God had just given to Jacob to resettle in his native land.

> I am the God of Bethel, where you anointed a pillar and where you made a vow to me. Now leave this land at once and go back to your native land. (Genesis 31:13)

By living outside Shechem, was Jacob already in a place and among a people God had specifically directed him away from? As we'll see in this story, he is a passive father at best. Jacob not only failed to protect and defend his own daughter, but he also floundered in his ability to guide and control his sons.

Jacob's family members were wealthy landowners, something like prosperous Bedouin tribesmen, but they did not live in cities like the highly urbanized inhabitants of Canaan did. We know from archaeological evidence of this period that Canaanite cities were wealthy, well-populated centers of commerce, straddling the Fertile Crescent route between Mesopotamia and Egypt. Canaan was a crossroads of the world, and its various peoples were literate and culturally sophisticated. Their religion was decidedly pagan and polytheistic—a mishmash of gods from the region, including Ishtar and Baal, Chemosh and Bel. The monotheistic outsiders who arrived in their midst, living in camel-skin tents instead of buildings and worshipping an invisible mysterious god, must have appeared awfully strange to the Canaanites. At the same time, Jacob's children would have been fascinated by this new land in which they found themselves, and this strange new people.

It was against this backdrop that Jacob's only known daughter set out.

> Now Dinah, the daughter Leah had borne to Jacob, went out to visit the women of the land. When Shechem son of Hamor the Hivite, the ruler of that area, saw her, he took her and raped her. (Genesis 34:1-2)

In this horrific situation, a young woman was victimized by a man who apparently had zero regard for her as a person. Dinah was likely a young teenager when she was brutalized. Jacob and his family were living in a land where they were outsiders, in a culture where young women could be seen as "fair game" by ungodly men. Did Jacob fail in his parental duty to supervise and protect her? It appears she felt no fear in venturing out alone. Did her parents know she had set out by herself?

Any woman who has ever suffered sexual violence can understand the kind of suffering that Dinah went through. For many women, the psychological toll can be even more destructive than the physical one. To undergo the violation of our bodies at the most intimate level tears at the fabric of our being. There can be enormous healing in turning to qualified, compassionate professionals to walk a victim through the trauma. A support network of trusted loved ones can also help a woman weather the flood of emotions, from anger to despair. God Himself promises to bind up our wounds, to be close to the brokenhearted and save those "who are crushed in spirit" (Psalm 34:18). The process of recovery and forgiveness can be long and agonizing, but it is possible. Survivors themselves are often the most empathetic advocates, able to turn their tragedy into a path that guides others to wholeness.

Dinah had only known the protection of her family's tents and the respect accorded women in a culture in which all members of the family worked side by side. Any woman's shock at being treated like an object, like a commodity to be abused and then thrown aside, is severe. Dinah's would have been especially so as a country girl, an outsider—perhaps dangerously naive. She had gone from being her mother's treasured youngest child to being treated like a possession by a cruel, entitled man. Oddly enough, in victimizing Dinah, Shechem may actually have taken her specifically because she would be of value to him. Jacob was a wealthy man, and marriage to his daughter would have been beneficial. Shechem well knew that after he raped Dinah, it would likely be impossible for her family to arrange another honorable marriage for her.

There are many unpleasant things to try to digest in this story, including the passage that follows Dinah's rape.

> His heart was drawn to Dinah daughter of Jacob; he loved the young woman and spoke tenderly to her. And Shechem said to his father Hamor, "Get me this girl as my wife." (Genesis 34:3–4)

It seems the better description of Shechem's feelings toward Dinah is that they were fueled by lust, not love. Love does not forcibly violate a young woman. And what are we to make of the revelation that he "spoke tenderly" to her (Genesis 34:3)? Some abusers and rapists will attempt to sweet-talk their victims, whether to cover their own misdeeds or to convince the victim that they in some way consented or provoked the attack. We're told nothing about how Dinah felt or responded, only her rapist's selfish demand that she be made to marry him.

Then her father, Jacob, found out.

> When Jacob heard that his daughter Dinah had been defiled, his sons were in the fields with his livestock; so he did nothing about it until they came home. (Genesis 34:5)

What?! Your daughter has been raped, and you're just going to stand idly by until your sons get home? As we'll see a bit later,

Jacob often appeared (as his mother Rebekah did) to be more concerned about the potential impact of events on *him*, rather than on others. What's also missing in this story is any interaction between Jacob and Dinah. She was the daughter of his less-favored wife, Leah, after a long line of sons. What was their relationship like? Was he disconnected from her life and activities? At the moment he learned his daughter had been violated, this verse tells us Jacob "did nothing." Every daughter wants to feel her father is the protector and defender she can count on. Sadly, that's not always the case, and the Bible doesn't hide the flaws of the men and women God is otherwise able to use in His plans—like Jacob.

Shechem's father, Hamor, approached Jacob to talk about what had happened. Hamor was a leader over the region, with authority and power. In those days, sexual conduct was less about consent than it was cultural norms and appearances. It looks like the father of Dinah's rapist thought the best way to handle the crime was to clean it up by negotiating a marriage for his entitled son . . . and then her brothers found out.

> **Meanwhile, Jacob's sons had come in from the fields as soon as they heard what had happened. They were shocked and furious, because Shechem had done an outrageous thing in Israel by sleeping with Jacob's daughter—a thing that should not be done. (Genesis 34:7)**

The narrator of Genesis made it clear, more than once, what happened was abominable: "outrageous," "should not be done." Take notice of the phrase "in Israel." For the very first time in the Bible, "Israel" refers not to a man, Jacob, the son of Isaac and Rebekah, but to a people. And when a crime had been committed, it had been committed "in Israel," as though this little band of God-fearing outsiders was a mighty and unified people. Dinah's rape created for the first time this sense that they were not just Jacob's family, but also the people of Israel. It was in response to injustice that Abraham's descendants truly became Israel. The danger came when a quest for justice veered into vengeance, as we'll soon see.

Not once does the text record Jacob or any of his sons questioning whether this rape had actually happened, or—more significantly—questioning whether Dinah had consented or not. Dinah had no reason to doubt that she would be avenged, and that the community of her family would have her back 100 percent. Survivors of sexual violence frequently express that one of the most important things that helped them get through their trauma was someone believing their story. Dinah's family did not even need to have the conversation; their belief in her, and in Shechem's guilt, was absolute. They did not sit down to have a debate about whether Dinah should or should not have been going out visiting that day anyway. The Bible does not comment on her behavior in any way at all. That was irrelevant to what happened to her; Shechem raped her. The Bible examines his sin, and he is the one held accountable—ferociously so, by her infuriated brothers.

The immediate reaction from Dinah's brothers was rage, which was a marked contrast to Jacob's seemingly blasé acknowledgment of what had happened. Here's where this story gets so far afield from how our current culture operates that it's hard to fathom. The father of Dinah's rapist began negotiations with Jacob.

But Hamor said to them, "My son Shechem has his heart set on your daughter. Please give her to him as his wife. Intermarry with us; give us your daughters and take our daughters for yourselves. You can settle among us; the land is open to you. Live in it, trade in it, and acquire property in it." (Genesis 34:8-10)

One red flag after another. Not only did Shechem's father want Dinah to marry his son, but the request was also made in a way that suggested there was some love affair going on. Then Jacob was presented with a much broader point of compromise: *let's just start intermarrying!* Jacob, whose twelve sons were the foundations of the tribes of Israel, was presented with the suggestion that he play fast and loose with the covenant God had made directly with his family.

As the conversation continued, Shechem himself spoke up:

Then Shechem said to Dinah's father and brothers, "Let me find favor in your eyes, and I will give you whatever you ask. Make the price for the bride and the gift I am to bring as great as you like, and I'll pay whatever you ask me. Only give me the young woman as my wife." (Genesis 34:11-12)

Jacob is described here as "Dinah's father." That's notable because one of the key duties of a father in the Ancient Near East was to negotiate marriages for their daughters. But try to imagine the man who had violated your daughter or sister saying, "Let me find favor in your eyes." Was Dinah's value as a young woman so inconsequential to Shechem and his family that they believed the crime against her could simply be bartered away? Shechem essentially put a price on her head. *Just name your cost, and let me have her.* Shechem becomes an even more repellent figure when you remember that during all this negotiation, while Shechem is smiling and making nice with her family, Dinah is still being held prisoner.

THE FAMILY'S RESPONSE

Whatever Jacob was thinking at this point doesn't seem to matter. His sons had already decided that they didn't owe any shred of honor or integrity to Shechem or his father, Hamor. So Simeon and Levi conned the people of Shechem, and the deal they made would end in death and destruction.

> They said to them, "We can't do such a thing; we can't give our sister to a man who is not circumcised. That would be a disgrace to us. We will enter into an agreement with you on one condition only: that you become like us by circumcising all your males. Then we will give you our daughters and take your daughters for ourselves. We'll settle among you and become one people with you. But if you will not agree to be circumcised, we'll take our sister and go." (Genesis 34:14–17)

Jacob himself was the original trickster, the wily negotiator and crafty plotter—a man who betrayed his own twin brother, Esau, and father, Isaac. It would make sense that the revenge his sons cooked up was as devious and as clever as their father's. He had taught them well. Note that the brothers, in what I'm sure they believed was justified deception, offered up circumcision as a part of their scheme. Circumcision was the mark of Abraham's covenant with God, a symbol of the commitment to live as His people. It was a continual physical reminder that God had created a nation out of His unblemished promises. Here Jacob's sons were using something meant to be holy as a negotiating ploy, a means of vengeance—and Shechem and Hamor bought it.

Their proposal seemed good to Hamor and his son Shechem. The young man, who was the most honored of all his father's family, lost no time in doing what they said, because he was delighted with Jacob's daughter. So Hamor and his son Shechem went to the gate of their city to speak to the men of their city. "These men are friendly toward us," they said. "Let them live in our land and trade in it; the land has plenty of room for them. We can marry their daughters and they can marry ours. But the men will agree to live with us as one people only on the condition that our males be circumcised, as they themselves are. Won't their livestock, their property and all their other animals become ours? So let us agree to their terms, and they will settle among us."

All the men who went out of the city gate agreed with Hamor and his son Shechem, and every male in the city was circumcised. (Genesis 34:18–24)

What a great deal for the family of the man who'd violated Dinah. It's hard to miss the continued references to Shechem's position as "honored" or "favored." He was basically the equivalent of a prince, and I'd guess princes were used to getting what they wanted. Shechem would not only get to keep Dinah, but his people stood to benefit financially from this arrangement. Greed was clearly a part of this deal, on many levels. Shechem and Hamor must have been convincing, though, because all of the men of their community agreed to the painful process of circumcision.

Everything I've studied or heard on the issue of circumcision in adult males cites day three after the procedure as the most painful in the recovery process. Would the men have been relying on alcohol or another mind-altering substance to help dull the pain? Whatever the facts on the ground, two of Jacob's sons timed their attack to find the men at their most vulnerable and carry out a merciless slaughter.

> Three days later, while all of them were still in pain, two of Jacob's sons, Simeon and Levi, Dinah's brothers, took their swords and attacked the unsuspecting city, killing every male. They put Hamor and his son Shechem to the sword and took Dinah from Shechem's house and left. The sons of Jacob came upon the dead bodies and looted the city where their sister had been defiled. They seized their flocks and herds and donkeys and everything else of theirs in the city and out in the fields. They carried off all their wealth and all their women and children, taking as plunder everything in the houses. (Genesis 34:25–29)

Simeon and Levi, Dinah's brothers, went total scorched earth. They not only killed her rapist and his father, but every man in the city. They plundered everything they could get their hands on. Yes, they took back Dinah, but they also took every other woman and child too. There was a breaking point when Jacob's sons clearly ran way past justice and into the bloodthirsty rage of all-out vengeance.

You'll often hear reference to the idea of Old Testament justice as "an eye for an eye" and so on. Some have interpreted that to mean you can mete out punishment in the same measure of what's been lost. The Latin words *lex talionis* translate into "law of retaliation." The concept wasn't meant to unleash violence or revenge. It's actually about reining it in or setting a maximum limit of how far someone could go in paying back the one who'd damaged them, not a minimum. It's the idea of letting the punishment fit the crime. Simeon and Levi did no such thing. They left absolutely no room for any measure of mercy.

Our heavenly Father is well versed in the concept of deciding when to grant leniency, whether we humans deserve it or not. In his prayer, the prophet Habakkuk appealed to God on behalf of the people.

> LORD, I have heard of your fame;
>> I stand in awe of your deeds, LORD.
>> Repeat them in our day,
>> in our time make them known;
>> in wrath remember mercy. (Habakkuk 3:2)

Many times, God did choose to redeem His people rather than crush them. The entire New Testament is about His decision to give up His own Son so that sinners who could never be perfect enough would have a grace-filled path to reconciliation with God. One of Jesus's most well-known parables is also one of his most convicting. In Matthew 18, after Peter asked Jesus how many times we must forgive those who sin against us, Christ told the story of a man who was deep in debt. He was called before a king who wanted to settle accounts with his servants.

> As he began the settlement, a man who owed him ten thousand bags of gold was brought to him. Since he was not able to pay, the master ordered that he and his wife and his children and all that he had be sold to repay the debt. At this the servant fell on his knees before him. "Be patient with me," he begged, "and I will pay back everything." The servant's master took pity on him, canceled the debt and let him go. (Matthew 18:24-27)

One estimate calculates the amount this servant owed as equivalent to nearly $3.5 billion dollars—with a *b*. There was absolutely zero chance the man could have ever paid it back, just like the debt created by our sins. Yet instead of being overcome with gratitude, what did the man do?

> But when that servant went out, he found one of his fellow servants who owed him a hundred silver coins. He grabbed him and began to choke him. "Pay back what you owe me!" he demanded. His fellow servant fell to his knees and begged him, "Be patient with me, and I will pay it back." But he refused. Instead, he went off and had the man thrown into prison until he could pay the debt. (Matthew 18:28-30)

Hold up. The servant who'd just had a multibillion dollar debt wiped clean then went and took a man who owed him roughly

$5,800 and had him thrown in prison? Correct, but he wasn't going to get away with it.

> When the other servants saw what had happened, they were outraged and went and told their master everything that had happened. Then the master called the servant in. "You wicked servant," he said, "I canceled all that debt of yours because you begged me to. Shouldn't you have had mercy on your fellow servant just as I had on you?" In anger his master handed him over to the jailers to be tortured, until he should pay back all he owed. This is how my heavenly Father will treat each of you unless you forgive your brother or sister from your heart. (Matthew 18:31–35)

If that's not convicting, I don't know what is. That parable is such a concrete example to me of how much undeserved mercy and grace I've been given, and the fact that I have zero standing to withhold forgiveness from others. Does God believe in justice? Yes, thank goodness, but He also calls us to factor in mercy. Simeon and Levi did not.

Where was Jacob in all of this? We're looking at the lives of daughters in this book, so what about Dinah and what about her father? How is it that Jacob says nothing in this story until *after* his daughter has been rescued—and in abominable fashion? Rather than recoiling in horror at what his sons had done, Jacob reacted by worrying about how their killing spree was going to impact *him*. Like mother, like son.

Then Jacob said to Simeon and Levi, "You have brought trouble on me by making me obnoxious to the Canaanites and Perizzites, the people living in this land. We are few in number, and if they join forces against me and attack me, I and my household will be destroyed."

But they replied, "Should he have treated our sister like a prostitute?" (Genesis 34:30–31)

Jacob was likely right that Simeon and Levi had put them all in danger. They were not yet a mighty nation. They wouldn't stand a chance against the combined forces of the Canaanite cities if those potential foes decided to wipe Jacob and his family off the map of the Middle East and out of history forever. But this was a Jacob who was tired of fleeing. He'd had to escape Canaan in fear for his life once before, and he'd fled Syria because his father-in-law, Laban, was hot on his trail. *Just once,* Jacob may have thought, *can I stay in a place without having to run away from it because people are trying to kill me?*

But it was time to go, to the place God had already directed Jacob to settle his family. Following the rape of his daughter and an ungodly massacre by his sons, Jacob was on the move again.

Then God said to Jacob, "Go up to Bethel and settle there, and build an altar there to God, who appeared to you when you were fleeing from your brother Esau."

So Jacob said to his household and to all who were with him, "Get rid of the foreign gods you have with you, and purify yourselves and change your clothes. Then come, let us go up to Bethel, where I will build an altar to God, who answered me in the day of my distress and who has been with me wherever I have gone." So they gave Jacob all the foreign gods they had and the rings in their ears, and Jacob buried them under the oak at Shechem. (Genesis 35:1–4)

It seems Jacob finally answered the wake-up call. He was willing to go where God directed him, and to truly honor Him. He commanded his family and everyone among their households to get rid of their false gods. How had that practice become acceptable? Jacob knew it was wrong and completely in conflict with God's covenant with Abraham, one that flowed to his descendants. How fitting that all of the idols were buried and left at Shechem.

Jacob would not forget what his sons had done. In his final words to his family, the patriarch made clear there would be consequences.

Then Jacob called for his sons and said: "Gather around so I can tell you what will happen to you in days to come.

"Assemble and listen, sons of Jacob;
listen to your father Israel. . . .
Simeon and Levi are brothers
their swords are weapons of violence.
Let me not enter their council,
let me not join their assembly,
for they have killed men in their anger
and hamstrung oxen as they pleased.
Cursed be their anger, so fierce,
and their fury, so cruel!

I will scatter them in Jacob
and disperse them in Israel." (Genesis 49:1-2, 5-7)

Ouch. In his dying breath, Jacob was still calling out his own sons. *I want no association with these two.* Jacob vowed Simeon and Levi would be scattered and dispersed, unlike the tribes/families of his other sons, who would grow and prosper together.

What eventually became of Simeon and Levi? As Moses was dying and blessing the tribes, he left out Simeon altogether (Deuteronomy 33). Joshua 19 tells us that Simeon's descendants were eventually given land, but it was *inside* the land apportioned to Judah's. Simeon's tribe continued to dwindle and was essentially subsumed into Judah's. Levi's descendants were given no land of their own (Joshua 18:7) and eventually went to Eleazar the priest to ask for somewhere to live. The Israelites eventually agreed to give them various towns where they could take up residence, but they were all throughout the nation—*dispersed*. In Joshua 21:21, we learn one of the cities Levi's descendants are allowed to settle in is Shechem, where this entire tragedy started. The brothers' disproportionate, vigilante justice cost them and their families for generations.

A Daughter's Ultimate Protector

The Bible does not give us a window into Dinah's inner dialogue or feelings about any of this. Yes, she is central to the story, but it appears the larger points are about several other themes: drifting away from what God had called Jacob to, the evil actions of a man who wasn't in covenant with God, and the deceit and deadly overreaction of men who were. Dinah was a young woman, traumatized and caught in the middle of an ugly dispute that turned into a massacre. We see a father who appears disconnected and ambivalent when it comes to his daughter, at moments when she needed him most. Jacob was an imperfect father, yet God honored the covenant He'd made with Abraham and used Jacob despite his inadequacies.

It is human nature to impose on our heavenly Father the experiences we as daughters have with our earthly fathers. We are all lacking, both as parents and children. So, it's important that we constantly refocus our relationship as daughters of God on the unwavering truths of His character. When others abandon, He is ever-present (Proverbs 15:3). When others condemn, He is full of compassion (Psalm 86:15). When others neglect, He is so attentive that He knows every single hair on our heads (Luke 12:7). When others tear down, He is our Healer (Psalm 147:3). When others are uninterested, He is waiting to listen to our fears and to give us peace in return (Philippians 4:6–7).

Lord God, grant us the courage of Dinah. Help us to create a culture in our families that honors and respects women. If we have daughters, show us how to make sure they know their worth every single day. If we have ever doubted our own value, remind us how infinitely precious we are to You, no matter what we have suffered in the past. Heavenly Father, make fresh in our minds Your redeeming love and endless grace. Please bind up our deepest wounds, grant us the courage to forgive, and show us how to be an agent of healing for others.

Dinah Study Questions

1. Why do you think Dinah's story is recorded in the Bible?

2. How should we in the modern church minister to and treat the victims of sexual violence? Have you or a loved one experienced an assault? If so, are you still dealing with the trauma? What resources have been most helpful? What do you wish the church understood about helping in the aftermath of sexual violation?

3. What do we know about what kind of father Jacob was—both to his sons and his daughters?

4. How did Shechem and his family view Dinah and her worth? (Genesis 34:11–12)

5. Were Simeon and Levi justified in deceiving Shechem and his family? What about their decision to use the sign of God's covenant with His people: circumcision?

6. What does Jesus clearly tell us about the concept of mercy in Matthew 18?

7. What were the long-term ramifications of Simeon's and Levi's actions for themselves and their descendants? (Genesis 49:1–2, 5–7; Joshua 18:7; 21:21)

8. How does our relationship with our earthly father influence how we view our heavenly Father? If our earthly father has been less than ideal, how does Scripture point us to the truth about God and how he views us as His children? (Proverbs 15:3; Psalm 86:15; Luke 12:7; Psalm 147:3; Philippians 4:6–7)

(Book of Esther)

ℭHE 𝒫RINCESS WITH A 𝒮ECRET

The book of Esther is unlike any other book of the Bible. It's a real-life story that's as captivating as a fairy tale: the journey of an ordinary peasant girl, whisked away to a palace to win the heart of the king. The story is not quite that simple and involves all sorts of grisly political and personal scheming, as well as ideas of marriage that are very different from our own. Esther is a love story. It's also about palace intrigue, and the miraculous rescue of God's people. But underlying all those things, it is a story first and foremost about family: Esther's family.

By contrast, the first act in the book is the picture of a family being torn apart. Xerxes, king of Persia, cast out his wife Queen Vashti for refusing to obey his commands. He then began the search for a new queen.

After the scene is set, we are presented with the real heroes of the story: Esther and Mordecai.

Now there was in the citadel of Susa a Jew of the tribe of Benjamin, named Mordecai son of Jair, the son of Shimei, the son of Kish, who had been carried into exile from Jerusalem by Nebuchadnezzar king of Babylon, among those taken captive with Jehoiachin king of Judah. Mordecai had a cousin named Hadassah, whom he had brought up because she had neither father nor mother. This young woman, who was also known as Esther, had a lovely figure and was beautiful. Mordecai had taken her as his own daughter when her father and mother died.

When the king's order and edict had been proclaimed, many young women were brought to the citadel of Susa and put under the care of Hegai. Esther also was taken to the king's palace and entrusted to Hegai, who had charge of the harem. She pleased him and won his favor. Immediately he provided her with her beauty treatments and special food. He assigned to her seven female attendants selected from the king's palace and moved her and her attendants into the best place in the harem.

Esther had not revealed her nationality and family background, because Mordecai had forbidden her to do so. Every day he walked back and forth near the courtyard of the harem to find out how Esther was and what was happening to her. (Esther 2:5–11)

Esther and Mordecai were not actually father and daughter. They were related by blood, but possibly only distantly. She is described as his "cousin," whom Mordecai had "taken . . . as his own daughter" because her father and mother had died (Esther 2:7). So immediately we learn that Mordecai was a kind man who saw a vulnerable child in need and acted. Repeatedly the Bible holds out to us the value of "found family," the idea that people not related by blood can still form deep bonds of care and community. The book of Esther shows us all the richness and blessing that can come from that kind of family. In the Bible, families of choice are never second best. Ruth and Naomi are just as much family as are Jochebed and Miriam. And these "found families" are an important model of the love and grace of God through His adoption of us, and our own choice of faithfulness to Him.

Adoption is something we're exceptionally grateful for in my family. My mother was adopted at the end of World War II, back in the late 1940s. Whatever the circumstances of her birth, she was welcomed into a family of love. My grandparents poured their lives into their two daughters, both adopted, and created a place of security. I spent much of my childhood with them. It was where I felt safest and most loved, watching *The Price Is Right* and eating cottage cheese and unsalted peanuts when I was home "sick" from school. Had my mother come along thirty years later, who knows what her biological mom would have chosen. Millions of women in America face unplanned pregnancies every year. How overwhelmed and frightened many of them must be, wondering if it's possible to gather the emotional support and financial resources they would need to raise a child. I've often pondered what my biological grandmother's situation was. Was she in trouble? Afraid? Overwhelmed? In any case, I'm thankful she made what must have been an excruciating decision: to give her daughter life and then to give her away. That selfless decision created the family I treasure. It just so happens my best friend is adopted too! It's a blessing to watch as many of my friends have expanded their families by embracing children in need at all stages of their young lives—just as Mordecai did for Esther.

At the end of the previous quoted passage we see two statements that illuminate the relationship between the pair. Mordecai forbade Esther from revealing to anyone that she was a Jew, and also every day he kept vigil outside the courtyard of the king's harem to find out how she was doing. What parent among us can fail to relate to Mordecai's watchfulness here? Pacing back and forth while waiting to hear how your loved one is doing is clearly a universal human experience. We see in this little snippet how Mordecai fulfilled the role of being a father to Esther, and just how deep his concern for her ran. Those of us with fathers who loved and cherished us when we were growing up know what it is to be warmed by that kind of protectiveness and care. Was Esther able to glance out the windows and see Mordecai there, keeping faithful watch over her? Surely his presence would have reassured and strengthened her.

In these Scriptures we see two important aspects of the father-daughter relationship: a father's protection, and a daughter's trust. The Bible tells us, in strong language, that Mordecai had "forbidden" Esther to reveal who she really was (Esther 2:10). For some reason he sensed either a danger or disadvantage in that piece of information being revealed, and he made it clear that Esther wasn't to divulge it. However that sounded to Esther, she didn't hesitate to follow Mordecai's guidance. Scripture tells us she hid her background specifically because that's what Mordecai had told her to do. She trusted him completely. Her obedience was a fruit of her trust. Mordecai and Esther model the qualities of mutual love and respect.

We also see that Esther's obedience wasn't isolated, that it was a lifetime habit:

But Esther had kept secret her family background and nationality just as Mordecai had told her to do, for she con-

tinued to follow Mordecai's instructions as she had done when he was bringing her up. (Esther 2:20)

Esther's obedience to Mordecai's instructions stands in stark contrast to the way this story started, with Queen Vashti's disobedience.

At this point in the narrative the journeys of Mordecai and Esther diverged, and each had separate adventures. Esther continued to enjoy success in the high-stakes game of becoming the king's next queen, advancing from one level to the next until finally the king was more attracted to her than to any of the others. Meanwhile, unbeknownst to Esther, Mordecai happened upon a plot to assassinate the king. In fact, it seemed to be indirectly because of Esther that he uncovered this plot, for it was while Mordecai was sitting at the palace gates waiting for word of his daughter that he overheard this conspiracy.

So while the two plots begin to follow separate trajectories here, the Bible emphasizes for us how much they spring from the relationship between father and daughter. Mordecai was in the position to know about the plot because of his vigil for Esther, while Esther continued to enjoy success because she was concealing her identity, just as Mordecai had instructed. Further, the Bible points out that she was following these instructions not just because they seemed wise to her, or because Mordecai had persuaded her to, but because this had been her habit from the time she was a child: she obeyed "just as she had done when he was bringing her up" (Esther 2:20). The trust and respect that Mordecai earned in her childhood were guiding Esther's life to a position of both safety and divine destiny.

It's often unpleasant as a parent to lay down the law with your children, and for kids it can be maddening to take direction when they see no purpose to the instruction. My six-year-old self was always trying to argue with my mom, though she clearly knew better. I didn't know what I didn't know! How many times in my adulthood have I thanked her for being "The Meanest Mom in the World"? I've lost count. While I may have stuck to the rules strictly out of a begrudging obedience all those decades ago, the older I get the more I appreciate the protective boundaries she built for me. Like all parents it's possible Mordecai got it wrong sometimes, especially since he had to learn on the job with his adopted daughter. But all the times he got it right served as building blocks of trust for the foundation of his relationship with Esther. That was what stayed with her, and her trust and obedience ended up saving not just her life, but also the lives of every Jew in the Persian Empire.

ESTHER'S LIFE IN DANGER

Esther had been chosen to be queen, but as she would soon discover that wouldn't guarantee her existence would be one solely of luxury and ease. Her primary source of trouble was the king's trusted counselor, Haman, who would make things even more complicated. Haman had a specific contempt for Mordecai, who refused to bow and grovel before him, as it appears most everyone else in the kingdom was willing to do.

To understand the deeper roots of the conflict that sparked between Mordecai and Haman, let's take a quick look back. Haman was an Amalekite (or Agagite), a people God had commanded the

Israelites to completely wipe out. After the Israelites had finished escaping across the Red Sea on their epic exodus out of Egypt, the Amalekites attacked them—unprovoked.

> Then the LORD said to Moses, "Write this on a scroll as something to be remembered and make sure that Joshua hears it, because I will completely blot out the name of Amalek from under heaven." Moses built an altar and called it The LORD is my Banner. He said, "Because hands were lifted up against the throne of the LORD , the LORD will be at war against the Amalekites from generation to generation." (Exodus 17:14–16)

More than once God reminded the Israelites to take note.

> Remember what the Amalekites did to you along the way when you came out of Egypt. When you were weary and worn out, they met you on your journey and attacked all who were lagging behind; they had no fear of God. When the LORD your God gives you rest from all the enemies around you in the land he is giving you to possess as an inheritance, you shall blot out the name of Amalek from under heaven. Do not forget! (Deuteronomy 29:17–19)

> Now go, attack the Amalekites and totally destroy all that belongs to them. Do not spare them. (1 Samuel 15:3)

But King Saul did not follow God's clear command.

He took Agag king of the Amalekites alive, and all his people he totally destroyed with the sword. But Saul and the army spared Agag and the best of the sheep and cattle, the fat calves and lambs—everything that was good. These they were unwilling to destroy completely, but everything that was despised and weak they totally destroyed.

Then the word of the LORD came to Samuel: "I regret that I have made Saul king, because he has turned away from me and has not carried out my instructions." Samuel was angry, and he cried out to the LORD all that night. (1 Samuel 15:8–10)

Ouch. It's not just the Lord's short-term disappointment that Saul had to face. As we see in the story of Esther, the failure to do what God had directed the Israelites to do meant a very real threat remained and then multiplied. Though Agag was ultimately killed by the prophet Samuel, some remnant of his lineage clearly remained—and Haman was a descendant of his—an Agagite. Throw in the fact that Mordecai and Esther are believed to be from Saul's family and you can see the cataclysmic showdown coming.

It's against this backdrop that we see Haman's utter contempt for Mordecai and Mordecai's unequivocal refusal to bow to Haman as commanded. Here's where the real plot of the story begins.

When Haman saw that Mordecai would not kneel down or pay him honor, he was enraged. Yet having learned who Mordecai's people were, he scorned the idea of killing only Mordecai. Instead Haman looked for a way to destroy all Mordecai's people, the Jews, throughout the whole kingdom of Xerxes. (Esther 3:5–6)

At this point in history, Persia was home to thousands of Jews who had been taken there as captives after the destruction of the temple. Over the years, many of these Jews became accustomed to the culture and, even though Jews were eventually freely permitted to return to their homeland, they chose instead to stay. In Persia they found themselves residents of a large and cosmopolitan empire with many opportunities for advancement, a value for education and learning, and a high tolerance for minority groups. Esther and Mordecai's family was one among those who had apparently found prosperity and assimilation in Persia. Esther's Hebrew name, the text tells us, was Hadassah, but the fact that she went by Esther shows us that this was a young girl who had grown up as Persian as she was Jewish.

Despite their assimilation into Persian society, Haman clearly had an ongoing hatred for the Jewish people—along with a plan to wipe them out. He planned to use his position, and the king's authority, to get it done.

Then Haman said to King Xerxes, "There is a certain people dispersed among the peoples in all the provinces of your kingdom who keep themselves separate. Their customs are different from those of all other people, and they do not obey the king's laws; it is not in the king's best interest to tolerate them. If it pleases the king, let a decree be issued to destroy them, and I will give ten thousand talents of silver to the king's administrators for the royal treasury."

> So the king took his signet ring from his finger and gave
> it to Haman son of Hammedatha, the Agagite, the enemy
> of the Jews. "Keep the money," the king said to Haman,
> "and do with the people as you please." (Esther 3:8–11)

By convincing the king that the Jewish people presented a threat to his rule, Haman locked in Xerxes's full backing to wipe them out. What a diabolical plan. Yet God was well aware of Haman's schemes, and through Esther's obedience to Mordecai's protective guidance she was perfectly placed in the center of God's rescue plan.

I was fortunate enough to essentially have two "dads" in my life, the second being my stepfather, Jasper. As a young girl, I can remember being eager to master the skill of bike riding like the other kids in my neighborhood and to get rid of those training wheels! I assumed it was just as easy as the big kids made it look, but I quickly found out there was a steep learning curve. Jasper was the one who took the time to jog alongside me up and down the block over and over so I could try to find the balance to steady myself and take off on my own. It was a much harder (and much less fun) task than I thought I'd signed up for. After many failed attempts and wipeouts I put my hands on my hips, looked squarely at Jasper, and said, "You're trying to kill me!" Of course, he wasn't, and he knew just how badly I wanted to figure this thing out. He wasn't about to let me give up, left sidelined while the other kids zipped down our street. He also wasn't going to leave me to my own devices, determined to get on that bike—possibly tumbling into traffic. So, Jasper stuck with me. He guided me and kept me moving forward. That's the protective heart of a father, and the dedication we see from Mordecai.

Esther became aware of the threat when Mordecai dressed in sackcloth and ashes—the traditional garb of mourning—and lay at the gates of the king's palace. It's fair to say this put the queen into an awkward position. Wearing sackcloth and publicly wailing at the gates of the palace could have been considered a legal form of protest. Sackcloth was actually banned inside the palace itself because only splendor and luxury were acceptable inside the gates. Maybe that's why Esther didn't know about the edict that had been sent out with the official blessing of King Xerxes: orders to destroy, kill, and annihilate every single Jew—young and old, including women and children. To top it off, attackers were free to plunder everything the Jewish people owned as well. Mordecai sent a copy of the murderous order to Esther, and asked her to step up and risk everything in an attempt to stop the massacre—go to the king. She must have been stunned and terrified at the news, but Esther also stopped to remind Mordecai (you know, just in case he'd forgotten) that to approach the king without being summoned would expose her to being executed on the spot. That kind of disobedience was not tolerated in the highly ritualized Persian court, and it was a risk she was not willing to assume . . . at least not yet.

One of the most important themes the book of Esther grapples with is the idea of obedience. Very early on, we learn Esther was raised to be an obedient daughter to Mordecai. Mordecai wanted from his daughter what all parents want for their children: a healthy respect for authority, in the hopes that this will keep them safe. Esther's deference to Mordecai created an adult whose instinct was to obey and to trust authority. So what was she to do when the person who first taught her obedience—her adoptive father—was asking her to disobey her husband, the king? Let's not forget how that worked out for Vashti.

Mordecai left no room for doubt. His instructions were clear. Esther had a duty not just to him, but to their entire community. But wasn't she also bound to obey her king and husband? For the first time in her sheltered life, Esther experienced a profound conflict of obligation. She was not only compelled to obey Mordecai, but she was also obligated to respect the king. How was she to discern which path to choose? Her worlds were colliding: the one she'd been cautioned to hide and the one that made her the most celebrated and revered woman in the kingdom.

As she struggled to resolve her growing internal conflict, Mordecai's response to Esther was devastating:

Do not think that because you are in the king's house you alone of all the Jews will escape. For if you remain silent at this time, relief and deliverance for the Jews will arise from another place, but you and your father's family will perish. And who knows but that you have come to your royal position for such a time as this? (Esther 4:12–14)

He started with a direct, pointed critique. *Oh, do you think you are somehow going to stay safe? Is your life more important to you than the future of your own people?* He confronted Esther with her initial instincts of cowardice and selfishness. I'm not blaming her; I can identify! We're born selfish, wired to be primarily concerned with our own safety and comfort. Which of us in Esther's position would really have thought differently, at least at first?

Parents are uniquely equipped to give us a reality check when we need it most, and that's what Mordecai did here. He asked Esther to see herself in the broader context of history, to imagine her critical role in the story of God's people. His high expectations for Esther called her to remember who she was and to accept the grave challenge divinely set before her.

In my life, my father, Ed, definitely didn't sugar-coat things. But he was deeply emotional about family heritage, often walking us through the names and dates of our ancestors. He wanted us to have an appreciation for where we'd come from, and to carry that forward with us in life. He was proud of our Irish heritage (where do you think I got my name?) and our deep roots as multigeneration Floridians. When I was growing up, he'd also take any chance to detour into neighborhoods where he'd once lived or worked as a young law enforcement officer. My brother, Eddy, and I would roll our eyes and say, "Not another trip down memory lane!" But as we got older we came to understand and appreciate what our father was doing. He wanted to remind us of our roots, to keep us tethered to things that mattered, no matter where life took us. Mordecai did the same for Esther, pointing her to who she really was and how that fact equipped her to do something extraordinary.

And like Mordecai my father never wanted us to rest on our laurels. I can distinctly remember the morning after I'd placed in the top ten at Miss America, excited about the achievement but disappointed I'd lost. We were sitting at breakfast, having a chat. My dad was proud, but he also didn't want me to plateau at this first big milestone in my life. He said, "Don't let this be the most exciting thing that happens in your life." In a way I can hear Mordecai saying something similar to Esther. *Okay, so you won a beauty pageant. You've got a much bigger assignment now, so get to it!*

At Mordecai's reproof, Esther rose to the occasion:

Then Esther sent this reply to Mordecai: "Go, gather together all the Jews who are in Susa, and fast for me. Do not eat or drink for three days, night or day. I and my attendants will fast as you do. When this is done, I will go to the king, even though it is against the law. And if I perish, I perish."

So Mordecai went away and carried out all of Esther's instructions. (Esther 4:15–17)

All of a sudden, Esther was jolted into remembering her true self—her Jewish heritage, not her Persian stardom. In the beginning of the story, we saw that Esther was a young woman of two names: her Hebrew name Hadassah and her Persian name Esther. It was the Persian part of Esther that was so concerned with appearances, with paying honor to civil authority above all else, with worrying about what would happen to her personally. But it only took a few well-aimed words from her adoptive father to remind her of who (and what) she really was.

At his best, that is what a father does. Mordecai was concerned not with Esther's temporary, earthly safety, but with the compelling task she'd been assigned. Good fathers remind us that we are more than what consumes us on a daily basis—worries about money, and career, and reputation. The best kind of father mirrors our relationship with our heavenly Father. A father will demand more of us than we think we have to give, and he will rejoice with us when we discover that we can do more than we thought we could. Just like Jasper and that pink Huffy Sweet Thunder bike I eventually mastered! And whether or not your relationship with your earthly father is a good one, never doubt that your heavenly Father is always cheering for you.

It is not an accident that the father-daughter relationship in the Bible that may best mirror the beauty and fulfillment of our father-like relationship with God is this adoptive relationship between Esther and Mordecai. Not all fathers and daughters are biologically related—just as we are grafted into our spiritual relationship with God. But Mordecai chose Esther, just like God chose us. Mordecai looked at this vulnerable, orphaned little girl and said, *I will take care of her.* Mordecai's humble earthly actions mirror the cosmic actions of God reaching into the world, in His choosing us. God could have simply given us life, like He did with the animals, the birds, the fish—but they are not sons and daughters of God. He is divinely invested in the lives of believers. God has made a way for us: first in His adoption of the people of Israel as His own family, and then in the adoption of all of us through Christ's sacrifice.

So: What did Esther do, once Mordecai had reminded her of who she really was? Her instructions were simple and clear:

Go, gather together all the Jews who are in Susa, and fast for me. Do not eat or drink for three days, night or day. I and my attendants will fast as you do. When this is done, I will go to the king, even though it is against the law. And if I perish, I perish. (Esther 4:16)

First, she gathered the community. Esther did not say, *Give me some time and space to figure this out myself.* She knew great power can come when a community is gathered together, assembled as the people of God. Not only that, but she also knew that on a human level she needed their strength and support. Never has this principle been more real to me than during the earliest days of the pandemic, when most of us were suddenly cut off from physically gathering together in our houses of worship. I had relished Sundays, knowing that however the world would beat me up during the week I was safe and with kindred spirits in those pews.

Watching services at home just wasn't the same for me. I was grateful the option was available but deeply missed singing together and sharing the burdens in a tangible way. Our communion—such as it was—consisted of saltine crackers and Pedialyte. When we finally ventured out to church at an event on the road in Dallas, Texas, I confessed what we had been using to humbly celebrate the Lord's Supper. A sweet church member assured me I wasn't alone. "Honey, we've been using sweet tea and Ritz crackers!" she said. It made me see that we were never alone (and chuckle). We really did have a community weathering the anxiety and fear together, and that's where Esther turned in her moment of deepest need. Scripture tells us that "where two or three gather in my name, there am I with them" (Matthew 18:20). The spiritual power that comes from the gathering of the community—wherever and however we may be dispersed at the moment—can exponentially increase our individual pleas.

Second, Esther specifically called on the people to fast. This can be a charged topic! There are many Christians for whom fasting is not a regular practice today. But it was crucial to the lives of God's people in the Old and New Testaments. Fasting was a sign of repentance and humility before God, a way of underscoring our complete dependence on Him. But it was also a way of cultivating deep focus. When the Christian community at Antioch was sending Barnabas and Paul out on their mission journey, they united their prayer with fasting:

> While they were worshiping the LORD and fasting, the Holy Spirit said, "Set apart for me Barnabas and Saul for the work to which I have called them." So after they had fasted and prayed, they placed their hands on them and sent them off. (Acts 13:2-3)

In this passage, we see fasting as not just an aspect of supplicatory prayer but of worship itself. Jesus Himself commended fasting (Matthew 17:21) and assumed that it was not a question of *if* His followers would fast, but *when* (Matthew 6:16). Fasting continued to be a part of the Christian tradition for hundreds of years, concentrated most famously not only in times before the festivals of Christmas (in Advent) and Easter (in Lent) but also on other occasions throughout the year. When performed as a community, fasting is and was an especially powerful spiritual tool, which Esther used to her advantage.

Abstaining from food is not in itself a holy activity. Plenty of people go without food for reasons of vanity, health, or poverty. It is only when fasting is dedicated to God in an intentional and meaningful way, and when the time that would have been spent on eating is spent instead in prayer, that fasting becomes powerful. Notice what Esther said: "I and my attendants will fast as you do" (Esther 4:16). Fasting was not something she asked the community to do on her behalf, but to do along with her.

Finally, note Mordecai's reaction to Esther's newfound courage and spiritual wisdom: "So Mordecai went away and carried out all of Esther's instructions" (Esther 4:17). At the beginning of the story, Esther obeyed Mordecai faithfully, following all his commands. But near the end of the story, their positions are reversed: Mordecai is the one following Esther's instructions. At their best, fathers instill confidence in their daughters. Yes, obedience is key before we're old enough to reason through difficult decisions for ourselves. Ultimately, though, the goal is to raise young women to know truth, to recognize when God has placed them in a position to act, and to teach them to call on the courage they'll need in the moment. Esther had the wisdom and bravery to meet her challenge when it arrived.

The Happy Ending

For Esther, everything hung in the balance. She had pledged to break the rules and go to the king once the period of fasting was completed, and now it was go-time. She donned her royal robes and headed to the king's court. Esther was resigned to her fate, convinced she was meeting her destiny head-on when she approached the king.

> When he saw Queen Esther standing in the court, he was pleased with her and held out to her the gold scepter that was in his hand. So Esther approached and touched the tip of the scepter. (Esther 5:2)

Here begins the happy ending of Esther's perilous journey. Not only was Xerxes glad to see Esther, but he also told her to ask for anything, "up to half the kingdom, it will be given you" (Esther 5:3).

Esther's predecessor, Queen Vashti, was banished by the king because of her lack of obedience to his commands. Esther, presumably, was chosen as a replacement at least in part because she was not only beautiful but also young and pliable. Mordecai had taught her the value of obedience growing up, making her well suited to be the king's companion. But her whole story hinged on the moment when Esther had to be *dis*obedient. She had to break the laws of the king's court. Part of understanding and embracing true obedience is knowing when to disobey one edict in order to comply with a different, higher call.

Esther disobeyed spectacularly, and it paid off. The king was pleased to admit her (and throughout the story the unspoken truth seems to be that the king is quite taken with her), and Esther's life was spared. Given the chance, she didn't ask for even a fraction of the kingdom. This wasn't about her; it was about her people. She invited the king to a banquet along with Haman. Xerxes immediately accepted the invitation, and when he showed up the king again asked Esther what *he* could do for *her*. Notice how the king was eager to obey Esther now! She must have had an air of command about her. The king's crush on his bride peeks through too in his desire to grant nearly anything she could wish.

She invited them both back to a banquet the next day. Was she nervous, stalling for time? The Bible doesn't tell us, but it's clear she had lulled Haman into a deep sense of security. He left that first feast "happy and in high spirits," but they quickly soured when he saw Mordecai refusing to acknowledge him or show any fear in his presence (Esther 5:9). We're told he burned with rage. He soothed himself by calling together his friends in order to brag about his wealth, his position, and the two invites he'd scored from the queen. When Haman unloaded his disgust for Mordecai, his wife and his friends advised him to build a giant gallows and hang the Jewish man in the morning.

If you've studied Esther's story, then you know the amazing twist that comes next. While Haman was dreaming of his dastardly plan, King Xerxes couldn't sleep at all. He asked that old record books be brought to him and read. It reminded him of Mordecai's role exposing an assassination attempt on the king. Xerxes asked how Mordecai had been honored and found that nothing had been done. Note also that Mordecai had never demanded a reward or recognition. He'd neither lodged a complaint with the palace guard, nor fired off an angry letter to Persian customer service. Had their positions been reversed, you better believe Haman would have handled it differently and we've got proof!

As the king began to think about how to adequately thank the man who'd saved his life, Haman had entered the palace courts. He was headed to the king to ask for permission to kill the man the king wanted to honor: Mordecai. When Xerxes asked Haman for ideas about celebrating someone special, Haman (of course!) assumed he was the VIP about to take the spotlight. So (of course!) he proposed an elaborate, very public display of appreciation. That meant Haman spent his day making sure Mordecai was decked out in a royal robe, on one of the king's horses as Haman led him through the streets telling people, "This is what is done for the man the king delights to honor!" (Esther 6:10)—you know, instead of killing him. Every time I read this passage I'm gobsmacked! Haman had spent so much of his time being outraged that Mordecai wouldn't give him the respect he demanded. There are few reversals in the Bible more poetic than this one, and we're not even close to being done.

Haman had just enough time to go home and complain to his wife again before it was time to return to the second banquet with Queen Esther. Here's where it really gets good. The king once again asked what he could do to make Esther happy. She responded by asking him to spare her life and the lives of her people. Imagine how confused Xerxes must have been at first. He asked who could have devised such a scheme, and this was Esther's moment. She pointed right at Haman and called him out on the spot. The king was so angered he walked out into the palace garden. While Xerxes was gone Haman began to beg Esther for his life, and he was literally falling onto the couch where she was seated as the king walked back into the room.

The king exclaimed, "Will he even molest the queen while she is with me in the house?" (Esther 7:8)

You guessed it: things were about to go from bad to worse for Haman. At that very moment, one of the king's servants piped up, *Just so happens there's this giant gallows at Haman's house that he made for Mordecai—you know, that guy who saved your life.* The king's direction was swift: use it for Haman. Y'all!

I have to believe there were very real, concrete moments of extreme fear for Esther all through this journey. Yet she had relied on the counsel of Mordecai, honoring him as an obedient daughter and brave truth-teller when it mattered most. No blockbuster movie would be complete without an epic reveal, and Esther had one.

> That same day King Xerxes gave Queen Esther the estate of Haman, the enemy of the Jews. And Mordecai came into the presence of the king, for Esther had told how he was related to her. The king took off his signet ring, which he had reclaimed from Haman, and presented it to Mordecai. And Esther appointed him over Haman's estate. (Esther 8:1–2)

The king seems delighted to have finally met his wife's family, and equally pleased to extend extravagant honors to Mordecai. The king gave Mordecai his highest seal of approval, his signet ring—which had previously belonged to Haman. Esther no longer had to worry about how her adoptive father was doing outside the palace gates. Together, Esther and Mordecai ushered in God's deliverance for His people.

While no royal decree could be undone, Xerxes allowed Mordecai to script another royal edict. He drafted one that not only gave the Jewish people the right to assemble and defend themselves, but it also allowed them to "annihilate" anyone who came against them and to take the attackers' possessions as their own. Couriers rode "fast horses especially bred for the king" (Esther 8:10), and they fanned out to make sure that the second decree got to the farthest reaches of the Persian empire. The retribution against Haman's family and against all those who had been poised to murder the Jews was total. God did not tolerate those who plotted against His people.

In the end Mordecai and Esther stood united, proud to be family. Again and again, the book of Esther offers us reflections of our own lives, our own selves, and our own families. We have seen how Mordecai offers us the ideal of an earthly father in his care and protection of Esther. We have also seen how in choosing to take in Esther, Mordecai points us to our heavenly Father, who has chosen to adopt us. Here at the end, Mordecai points us heavenward once again. As Mordecai and Esther gather joyfully before the throne of the king, united at last, we see the true end and goal of family life: reunion before that other, greater throne in heaven, where our own families will someday finally and truly be fulfilled as they were meant to be.

The book of Esther goes on to explain how all these events are the origin of the festival of Purim, celebrated by Jewish communities today throughout the world. The carnival atmosphere of Purim is unlike any other Jewish holiday. There is very little solemnity in Purim, and nothing of sorrow. It is all joy. The reading of the book of Esther in synagogues today is the center of Purim. Congregations shout, "Blessed be Mordecai!" and "Cursed be Haman!" at appropriate points in the story, and there are often skits and plays telling the story of Esther, with costumes and carnivals for children. Purim is pure unadulterated joy, because Purim means the survival of the Jewish people not just from the threat of Haman, but also from the threat of all the Hamans throughout the centuries who have sought to destroy God's people.

The last verse of Esther gives us a final glimpse at Mordecai's character. He didn't simply gloat or coast for the rest of his tenure as the king's most trusted adviser.

He worked for the good of his people and spoke up for the welfare of all the Jews. (Esther 10:3)

That possibility and commitment sprang up from one simple family: one father and one daughter, who always had each other's backs. Just as the love and mutual care of Jochebed and Miriam brought about the liberation of their people, so the love of Esther and Mordecai saved the Jews from destruction. God kept His promises to His people, through earthly parents and children committed to faithfulness long before the glorious end result was clear.

Lord God, give us Your joy. We know that our own families and relationships are not always perfect. May the devotion of Esther and Mordecai to each other spur us to appreciate our loved ones, especially when life is difficult. May we always hear Your word speaking to us, even when our own fears make it hard to hear. Give us Esther's boldness and Mordecai's faithfulness. Help us to open our arms to Your love and to the love of our family.

Esther Study Questions

1. How does Esther's story model the importance of family in the absence of biological parents?

2. Why did Mordecai tell Esther to hide her identity in the beginning of her story? (Esther 2:20) Is it ever okay to counsel the people under our care to be less than truthful?

3. What does Esther's story tell us about the long-term impact of failing to obey God's commands? (1 Samuel 15; Esther 3:5–6)

4. Why is it important for us to speak truth to those we love? (Esther 4:8–17) How difficult can this be within a family?

5. How important is a faith community when you're struggling with a tough decision or painful challenge? (Esther 4:16; Matthew 18:20) What is the role of fasting and prayer?

6. Does Esther's story give you confidence that God is perfectly placing you where He needs you to be as part of His perfect plan? How can you meet fear and doubt when the enemy tries to tell you otherwise?

MICHAL

(1 Samuel 15–16, 1 Samuel 18:20–28, 1 Samuel 19:10–17,
2 Samuel 3:12–16, 1 Samuel 31:1–6, 2 Samuel 6:1–23)

MICHAL THE DAUGHTER OF SAUL

When it comes to marriage, you aren't just getting a spouse; you're getting a family. I'm fortunate that when I married into the Bream clan I got dozens of new in-laws who are basically a dream come true. There are no undermining or sneaky plots from in-laws to disrupt my marriage. It's a family full of faith, delicious food, and adventures. They cheer each other on and make me feel like I've always been a part of their tight-knit, devoted family. Now imagine the complete opposite of this situation and that's where we start with the story of Saul, his daughter Michal, and her husband, David. It should actually bring us comfort how often the Bible highlights troubled families (and individuals) and God's ability to carry out His plans despite their flaws and sin.

This family had as much drama and intrigue as an episode of *Downton Abbey*. Michal was a woman who found herself torn between two kings, in the middle of a terrible family struggle between her father, King Saul, and her beloved husband, David. This daughter not only chose not to participate in her father's sin, but she also actually undermined his nefarious plans. Michal was forced to choose between loyalty to her father and the vows she had made to her husband, David. This wasn't a misunderstanding or gray area; Saul wanted to kill David—and tried multiple times! (Your in-laws are sounding pretty good right about now, right?)

It wasn't always that way between Saul and David. Saul was Israel's first king, the one they demanded from God. The prophet Samuel had tried to push back against the people's wishes for a king, but God assured Samuel He had a plan—and that included Saul as king. Like so many others in the Scripture, Saul had times when he followed the Lord closely and other times when he followed his own whims. As we mentioned in the history leading up to Esther's story, Saul directly disobeyed an order from God to wipe out the Amalekites. It was at that point we saw that God's hand of blessing over Saul was removed, and Saul became very troubled. We're told even Samuel, who had anointed Saul at God's direction, mourned over him. In the midst of Samuel's moping, God told him to get it together and go visit Jesse—a man with eight sons.

It's during the interaction between the prophet Samuel and Jesse that we get one of the most well-known verses about how God perceives people and how He expects us to view them. Upon seeing Jesse's eldest son Eliab, Samuel was impressed and thought Eliab was the one chosen by God to be Israel's next king.

But the LORD said to Samuel, "Do not consider his appearance or his height, for I have rejected him. The LORD does not look at the things people look at. People look at the outward appearance, but the LORD looks at the heart." (1 Samuel 16:7)

One by one Samuel looked over Jesse's sons, but God had not chosen any of them. Samuel asked Jesse if there were any more? Well, the father admitted, there was his youngest one out there tending sheep. Jesse had David brought in and God made it clear this was His choice.

So Samuel took the horn of oil and anointed him in the presence of his brothers, and from that day on the Spirit of the LORD came powerfully upon David. (1 Samuel 16:13)

God had chosen David, and Samuel had anointed him as the next king of Israel. Tiny issue: Saul still thought he was the king. Saul no longer had God's backing or guidance, but he was still ruling over the nation of Israel. As Saul struggled with his sometimes explosive emotions, his servants had the idea of getting a musician to play harp music for him, to calm him. Saul commanded them to find someone, and David was suggested.

One of the servants answered, "I have seen a son of Jesse of Bethlehem who knows how to play the lyre. He is a brave man and a warrior. He speaks well and is a fine-looking man. And the LORD is with him." (1 Samuel 16:18)

Saul sent for him, and we're told the first time they met that Saul so admired him he made David one of his armor-bearers. Saul asked Jesse for permission to keep David on, and whenever

Saul was troubled, David's harp music soothed him. David also became best friends with Saul's son, Jonathan.

So far so good for the future in-laws, right? Why wouldn't Saul want David to marry one of his daughters? At the time of Michal's first appearance in the Old Testament, David's star was on the rise in the court of King Saul. David had slain Goliath in spectacular fashion, he and had become the darling of Israel. And what started out as Saul's admiration for David had turned into a growing, dangerous jealousy. We read in 1 Samuel 18 that David was successful on every mission Saul gave him. So much so, that the people increasingly took notice.

> When the men were returning home after David had killed [Goliath], the women came out from all the towns of Israel to meet King Saul with singing and dancing, with joyful songs and with timbrels and lyres. As they danced, they sang:
>
> > "Saul has slain his thousands,
> > and David his tens of thousands."
>
> Saul was very angry; this refrain displeased him greatly. "They have credited David with tens of thousands," he thought, "but me with only thousands. What more can he get but the kingdom?" And from that time on Saul kept a close eye on David. (1 Samuel 18:6–9)

Saul also tried to kill David by throwing a spear at him as he played the harp in the royal court. Sometime after that Saul hatched a plan. He offered David his older daughter, Merab, in marriage in exchange for David's commitment to fight on Saul's behalf. If David were the king's son-in-law, then he would be bound to Saul by family obligation, and if Saul ordered him to go fight, David could not refuse. Perhaps Saul thought it would serve him better to let the Philistines take out David, instead of the king doing it himself. Did he also think it would be useful to have his daughter reporting back to him on David's movements, as well—a spy in his enemy's household? Of course, the tragedy is that David was not Saul's enemy; he had sought only to serve the king. Saul created his own enemy, and that eventually left David no choice but to move against him. David essentially turned down Saul's offer to marry Merab, responding that he and his family were too humble to join the royal family. So Saul married off his daughter to another man instead of David.

Now enter Saul's younger daughter Michal. She's the only woman I can remember seeing in the Bible who openly professes her love for a man. She had fallen hard for this handsome, successful warrior, but we never see any indication that David reciprocated her feelings. Michal's love for David, the Bible hints, was unrequited. And as we'll see, David's later actions appear to back this up. Saul had his servants reach out to David and offer a second chance to become the king's son-in-law. David again protested, "I'm only a poor man and little known" (1 Samuel 18:23). There's plenty of scholarly speculation out there about what was really going on. Was David concerned about his ability to pay a customary price for his bride? Was he worried about getting caught up in one of Saul's schemes? I mean, the man had tried to murder him! In any case, Saul saw a golden opportunity. He told David the only thing he wanted in return for Michal's hand in marriage was the foreskins of one hundred

Philistines. Yikes! Saul's motive was even worse than the barbaric request itself:

Saul's plan was to have David fall by the hands of the Philistines. (1 Samuel 18:25)

In a cunning ploy, Saul offered David a path to prove his worthiness by killing a hundred Philistines, which was a catch-22 offer worthy of an evil genius. If David said no, he risked looking like a coward in front of the very crowds that were exalting him for his heroism. But if he said yes, the odds were that he would be hurt or killed trying to bring down that many enemy warriors. From Saul's perspective, it was a win-win situation. There was a decent chance David would be killed fighting the Philistines, *but* there was also the possibility that Saul would be afforded esteem and honor if David survived and joined the royal family. Either way, Saul was hoping to neutralize the threat to his kingship.

I have to admit, my own husband, Sheldon, had suspicions that my dad was out to get him from the moment I first took him home to meet my family. My father was a big fan of pyrotechnics. He didn't need July Fourth in order to set off a near-professional display of fireworks. He relished getting his hands on the good stuff and looked for any excuse to light up the sky. The very first night Sheldon met my dad we had a cookout, and you better believe fireworks were part of the postdinner plan. As they started popping and crackling, something went wrong. One of the rockets tipped over and aimed right at Sheldon's head! As it whooshed by it hit the side of Dad's brick house behind Sheldon and exploded. As soon as it was clear Sheldon was unscathed, my dad doubled over in laughter and apologized profusely. Everyone else's shock quickly turned to chuckles too. My dad was slightly mortified, and we all knew his multiple apologies were genuine. That's because my dad loved me and consistently took actions to make sure I was happy, safe, and had everything I needed. Poor Michal had the antithesis of that in Saul.

Michal was crazy about David, and her father knew it. Yet he plotted to get the man killed. Saul had planned to use his older daughter as a pawn, and he was apparently willing to crush his younger daughter's heart too. How could a father be so selfish and completely unfazed by the enormous grief his direct actions could cause his own child? With no regard for his daughter's feelings, Saul hoped to take advantage of her love for David to finally push through a marriage.

If we can stop and look beyond the struggle between these two powerful men, we see Michal—really see her. It's not surprising that she would have fallen in love with David. After all, as a princess of the royal court she would have had a front-row seat to David's heroism when he took on Goliath. She would have been a witness to all his heroic exploits, and she would have lived alongside him at the court. David had become the close friend of her brother Jonathan, and he probably seemed like a member of the family already. He was a dashing, heroic young man who had saved her whole nation.

None of this mattered to Saul. He saw Michal's feelings only as a tactical advantage, and ruthlessly plotted to exploit them. Michal might have thought her father was doing a loving thing for her, when he proposed her marriage to David. Did she know—or suspect—that her father had ulterior motives? Saul wanted his daughter to be a "snare" to her husband (1 Samuel 18:21). He also wanted to use Michal to further endanger David. But once again God's spirit and protection were on David as he went out to fulfill the price Saul had requested for Michal's hand.

> So before the allotted time elapsed, David took his men with him and went out and killed two hundred Philistines and brought back their foreskins. They counted out the full number to the king so that David might become the king's son-in-law. Then Saul gave him his daughter Michal in marriage. (1 Samuel 18:24–27)

If Saul had feared the adulation people gave David before, then handing David yet another opportunity to prove himself as a warrior had not been a wise move. He must have thought it was worth it for the possibility that David would be killed in the process and his problem erased, but that wasn't what happened. David survived, his hero's luster burnished even more, and he married Michal. He was at last the king's son-in-law.

Being raised at the royal court, Michal probably witnessed not only David's exploits, but also her father's initial greatness and ensuing downward spiral. She very likely knew what kind of man her father was—or rather, the kind of man that her father's jealousy of David had turned him into. What a terrible thing it must have been, to watch the descent of her noble father into madness and evil. Saul was the king of Israel, a man chosen by the people and anointed by the prophet Samuel. He had had everything going for him—wealth, power, and the favor of God—and then he lost it by his own disobedience and poisonous jealousy. How difficult that must have been for Michal to watch.

Michal experienced the tragic pain of watching a loved one drift irrevocably away, and she likely experienced a deep sense of powerlessness. There probably wasn't anything she could have done or said to recall her father to health and wholeness. How difficult it is to be the child of a parent who is making destructive choices. Parents are usually authority figures for us, so what do we do when a parent becomes the one who needs guidance or some straight talk? There would be real friction between Saul and Michal, but not just yet. First, the celebration of a wedding.

MICHAL THE WIFE OF DAVID

If Michal had been hoping that her marriage would ease her father's irrational hatred of David, she was soon disappointed.

> When Saul realized that the LORD was with David and that his daughter Michal loved David, Saul became still more afraid of him, and he remained his enemy the rest of his days. The Philistine commanders continued to go out to battle, and as often as they did, David met with more success than the rest of Saul's officers, and his name became well known. (1 Samuel 18:28-30)

Saul apparently realized that his plan to use Michal against David was not going to work. She persisted in her love of her husband, though once again—perhaps tellingly—nothing is said of David's feelings toward her. Instead of softening his attitude toward her husband, her father was now confirmed in his hatred, and had become, in the chilling phrase, "his enemy the rest of his days" (1 Samuel 18:29). David continued to flourish, as did his good fortune in battle. Michal's father continued sinking into sin and despair.

Even though David's relationship with his father-in-law continued to deteriorate, his bonds with the rest of Saul's family became even closer. Michal was devoted to David, and his friendship with Saul's son Jonathan was deeply rooted. Jonathan even tried to advocate for David with his father, assuring Saul that David had no designs on the throne and was no threat to him. But Saul was too far gone in his jealousy to believe it. Once again Saul tried to kill David. There would be no reconciliation.

> Saul sent men to David's house to watch it and to kill him in the morning. But Michal, David's wife, warned him, "If you don't run for your life tonight, tomorrow you'll be killed." So Michal let David down through a window, and he fled and escaped. Then Michal took an idol and laid it on the bed, covering it with a garment and putting some goats' hair at the head.
>
> When Saul sent the men to capture David, Michal said, "He is ill."
>
> Then Saul sent the men back to see David and told them, "Bring him up to me in his bed so that I may kill him." But when the men entered, there was the idol in the bed, and at the head was some goats' hair. (1 Samuel 19:11–16)

Torn between the man who gave her life and the man she loved, Michal chose to protect her husband. She must have known of Saul's wickedness and his numerous attempts to kill her husband—both directly and indirectly. Not only did she help her husband escape, but Michal also cooked up her own scheme to give David a head start on his getaway.

Her father was displeased, but when he confronted Michal, she wasn't ready to take credit for exactly what she'd done.

> Saul said to Michal, "Why did you deceive me like this and send my enemy away so that he escaped?"
> Michal told him, "He said to me, 'Let me get away. Why should I kill you?'" (1 Samuel 19:17)

Now that her husband had safely gone, Michal could pretend that she had been on her father's side all along. David, she claimed, had threatened to kill her! It would have been an easily believable lie. Saul would likely believe the worst of the man who'd become the center of his obsessions. So David escaped and Michal was also safe—back in the palace, where her deception was unknown and everyone assumed her real loyalty was to her father. Michal did not consent to participate in her father's sin of attempted murder, and thus saved him from the greater sin of actual murder. Michal saved David that night, but she also saved Saul.

Politically, Michal was caught between being the daughter of the king and the wife of the (presumed) future king. It was not only a dangerous place to be, but also an emotionally harrowing one. Michal was torn between her father and her husband. It seems neither of them loved her in return, nor showed regard for her intrinsic value as a human being or a woman. Her father used her as a pawn in his war with David and gave her no further thought. The Bible tells us nothing of her husband's feelings for her, even though she saved his life. Just as in Esther's story, with Michal we see a daughter presented with a very difficult choice: whom to follow? Esther chose to be loyal to her Jewish father, instead of to a pagan king. But Michal was left with what probably felt like a no-win situation. On the one hand an evil father who was hell-bent on killing her husband, and on the other hand a husband who didn't seem to return the love she showered on him.

Unfortunately, Saul's scheming regarding his daughter's life continued. When next we hear of Michal, Saul has treated her marriage to David as though it did not exist. In fact, Saul married her off to another man! We have no indication that Saul ever sought Michal's feelings on the matter. The Bible tells us simply, "Saul had given his daughter Michal, David's wife, to Paltiel son of Laish, who was from Gallim" (1 Samuel 25:44). David had also taken a new wife—two of them, in fact. While in hiding with his men in the wilderness, slowly gathering more forces loyal to him, David married Abigail, widow of the wealthy Nabal, as well as Ahinoam of Jezreel. Michal's love story with David appears to have ended—the husband of her dreams gone from the palace, collecting other wives, and no prospect of their reunion because her father had married her off to someone else.

Likely none of us have experienced what it is like to be the daughter of a king married to someone vying to become the future king. But many of us do know what it is like to experience tension between the family we were born into and the family we establish. Conflict between fathers-in-law and sons-in-law is as old as human history. Fathers want to protect their daughters, and they often regard outsiders with suspicion—hopefully because they want the best for their child, not because they are murderous connivers like Saul. How many of us have made some of the same emotional choices Michal did? She did not invite conflict with her father. She did not defy him. She did not say, *I love David and there's nothing you can do about it!* She was careful not to antagonize her father. In Michal's case, that was because her father could have had her put to death for such defiance. In our own lives, being estranged from our family can feel like a death. Often it is the shrewder choice to avoid antagonizing anyone, and for women, that is something many of us are taught from a young age. It is often assumed our role is to make peace in a family, to make sure everyone is getting along. At its best, that can be a beautiful affirmation of the vocation of womanhood. At its worst, that expectation can place an unfair emotional burden that means we end up internalizing everyone's conflict.

Michal tried to have it both ways, but it's hard to see what other options she had. If she had chosen David she would have had to flee with him. There would have been no one to divert the soldiers and give David those crucial hours in which to make his escape. David might have been caught and killed. But if she had chosen Saul, it likely would have meant David's death. The only way Michal could maintain her loyalty to her husband was by appearing to be loyal to her father. It seems she made the best of an impossible situation.

As life unfolds, we sometimes find ourselves with circumstances that defy a simple answer. That is when I place myself at God's feet. Not only to cast my cares on Him as He instructs us to do in 1 Peter 5:7, but also because He is the ultimate source of wisdom.

If any of you lacks wisdom, you should ask God, who gives generously to all without finding fault, and it will be given to you. (James 1:5)

When we're caught between people we love, prayer and heavenly wisdom are two of our best tools. No one wants to be in these situations, but they do arise. Seek the Lord's guidance and He will be faithful to guide you through life's most challenging decisions. I also often turn to more mature Christians, people with life experience and a track record of being trustworthy. Their insights can offer valuable advice when you most desperately need it.

No Longer a Daughter

If Michal's heart wasn't already broken, after being used by her father and essentially abandoned by David, she was about to face an even more bitter twist. Saul was killed in a disastrous defeat. His son Ish-Bosheth ascended to the throne, propped up by Saul's cousin and general, Abner. But then David finally caught a break: Abner defected to David, and he agreed to swing the war in David's favor. For Abner to prove his intentions, David asked one thing of the general:

> "Good," said David. "I will make an agreement with you. But I demand one thing of you: Do not come into my presence unless you bring Michal daughter of Saul when you come to see me." Then David sent messengers to Ish-Bosheth son of Saul, demanding, "Give me my wife Michal, whom I betrothed to myself for the price of a hundred Philistine foreskins." (2 Samuel 3:13–14)

David's request was a shrewd one. If Abner was going to defect, he needed to show David that he meant it. He needed to show David that even if he wanted to, he could not go back to

Ish-Bosheth. What would be one thing that would prove that? Taking Michal, Saul's "possession," from right under his son's nose and leading her back to David. Michal was clearly the emotional battleground on which this battle between David and Saul was fought. In the list of Saul's unjust actions, this shows us that maybe it was taking Michal away from him that rankled David the most. The stage seems set for a romantic and loving reunion between David and Michal. But what happened was far more disturbing than that.

> So Ish-Bosheth gave orders and had her taken away from her husband Paltiel son of Laish. Her husband, however, went with her, weeping behind her all the way to Bahurim. Then Abner said to him, "Go back home!" So he went back. (2 Samuel 3:15–16)

Poor Paltiel! His reaction to losing his wife is the mirror of Michal's love for David in earlier chapters. It's heartbreaking to read. This is the only time in the Bible that we see a man weeping like this for the love of his wife. And it happens here, of all places! Did Paltiel have a choice in his marriage to Michal, any more than Michal did? It is impossible for us to know. But he seems devastated here, and his powerlessness in the face of the larger events reminds us of the human cost of scheming and sin.

Once again, Michal was treated like a pawn. Did she enjoy a few years of happiness with Paltiel? Or was she still yearning for David? The Bible offers us an interesting commentary on love here. Sometimes love is reciprocated, but sometimes human love is directed at someone who can't or won't love us in the way we desire. The Bible shows us people living real lives with real, complicated human emotions. The love of Michal for David, and the love of Paltiel for Michal, shows us that ordinary human yearning has a place in the Bible too.

There's so much we cannot know about Michal. Was she pleased to marry another man when she realized that David wasn't coming back for her—and that he had taken other wives? Or was she heartbroken by being used by her father yet again? Given the chance to return to the palace and assume the position of queen, was she all too eager to leave Paltiel and return to David? In those days, Michal may have had none of the autonomy necessary to make those decisions, and we're left to wonder about how she felt about being shuttled between households and relationships.

Michal experienced so much instability in her life: her father's shaky mental health, the uncertainty of his reign, the insecurity of her own marriage. With David's final victory, the balance of power shifted. But because her life was tied to both her father and her husband, the rise of one meant inevitably the fall of the other—and more anguish for Michal. David was able to move into a position of power and demand his wife back because the leaders of the house of Saul, the king and his son Jonathan, had already been killed:

> Now the Philistines fought against Israel; the Israelites fled before them, and many fell dead on Mount Gilboa. The Philistines were in hot pursuit of Saul and his sons, and they killed his sons Jonathan, Abinadab, and Malki-Shua. The fighting grew fierce around Saul, and when the archers overtook him, they wounded him critically.

Saul said to his armor-bearer, "Draw your sword and run me through, or these uncircumcised fellows will come and run me through and abuse me."

But his armor-bearer was terrified and would not do it; so Saul took his own sword and fell on it. When the armor-bearer saw that Saul was dead, he too fell on his sword and died with him. So Saul and his three sons and his armor-bearer and all his men died together that same day. (1 Samuel 31:1–6)

What an unimaginably devastating loss for Michal. On the same day, she lost her father and three of her brothers, including Jonathan. The personal loss must have felt overwhelming, even without considering the political power struggle going on in her country. No matter what her disagreements were with her father—and they were profound—Saul was still her father, and he afforded her the protection of being a princess of Israel. There was always the possibility of repentance, that he would come back to himself and repent of the wrong he had done against David and Michal. But with Saul's death, all possibility of repentance was gone, along with any protection she might have had.

It is as though the sin of murder that Michal's deception had prevented earlier came to fruition here. The irony is that Saul had been longing to commit murder for years, and he had attempted to kill David many times. He was ultimately unsuccessful, and Saul himself ended up being the target. Michal was in no position to save him. Saul's greatest victim was always, in the final analysis, himself. His efforts to use Michal—and others—to elevate himself had finally failed for good.

No Longer a Wife

So Michal was returned to David, as a sign of his final triumph over the house of Saul. What the personal state of their relationship was, the Bible does not tell us. We have no window into the conversations that took place between David and Michal until a few years later, when David finally retrieved the Ark of the Covenant and brought it in triumph to the temple in Jerusalem. For the first time since we were told of her love for David, we see Michal's feelings.

Now King David was told, "The LORD has blessed the household of Obed-Edom and everything he has, because of the ark of God." So David went to bring up the ark of God from the house of Obed-Edom to the City of David with rejoicing. When those who were carrying the ark of the LORD had taken six steps, he sacrificed a bull and a fattened calf. Wearing a linen ephod, David was dancing before the LORD with all his might, while he and all Israel were bringing up the ark of the LORD with shouts and the sound of trumpets.

As the ark of the Lord was entering the City of David, Michal daughter of Saul watched from a window. And when she saw King David leaping and dancing before the LORD, she despised him in her heart.

They brought the ark of the LORD and set it in its place inside the tent that David had pitched for it, and David sacrificed burnt offerings and fellowship offerings before the LORD. After he had finished sacrificing the burnt offerings and fellowship offerings, he blessed the people in the name of the LORD Almighty. Then he gave a loaf of bread, a cake of dates and a cake of raisins to each person in the whole crowd of Israelites, both men and women. And all the people went to their homes. (2 Samuel 6:12–19)

This moment, more than any other, symbolized David's final triumph as king of Israel. His military successes were one thing, but this showed that he truly had the favor and blessing of God. He went so far as to bless the people in God's name, acting in an almost priestly capacity. He blessed them "in the name of the LORD of Heaven's Armies" or the Lord of Sabaoth, as older translations render it (2 Samuel 6:18). It was a way of referring to God as the commander of the armies of angels, just as David himself was commander of the armies of men. The message was clear: as above, so below. God was king in heaven, and David was king on earth, a parallel of the divine king.

Clearly, Michal did not approve of David's spirited dancing or of his less-than-formal wardrobe choice. The Bible indicates that she was "filled with contempt." It would have been hard for any onlooker not to contrast David's exultation and joy in God with Saul's disobedience and estrangement. God, after all, had withdrawn His favor from Saul back when Saul had disobeyed him. And how had Saul transgressed? By assuming a religious role that was not his to assume. When the armies of Israel were about to go into battle against the Philistines, Saul offered the sacrifices to God in the sight of all his army so that they would not lose heart while they waited for Samuel to show up (1 Samuel 13:1–14). But Saul also followed up this ceremonial transgression by lying about its purpose. Saul had told Samuel he wished to seek the Lord's favor, but it seems his real motivation was fear of the people. In contrast, David's sacrifices were an expression of his faith, offered with joyful abandon.

Just a couple of chapters later, Samuel reminded us of what matters most when he chided Saul for, once again, failing to obey God's directions.

> Does the LORD delight in burnt offerings and sacrifices
> as much as in obeying the LORD?
> To obey is better than sacrifice,
> and to heed is better than the fat of rams.
> For rebellion is like the sin of divination,
> and arrogance like the evil of idolatry.
> Because you have rejected the word of the LORD,
> he has rejected you as king. (1 Samuel 15:22–23)

Did Michal struggle to understand what may have looked to her like real inconsistency? God had punished Michal's father for pushing his kingly way into matters of religion, telling him that he would one day lose his kingdom for his transgressions. Yet here was David, her husband, assuming a religious role at the head of the procession of the Ark. No fire came from heaven to smite him. He was the favored of God. Meanwhile Michal's father and brothers were dead, her family bereft of the kingdom. The injustice of it must have rankled her and filled her heart with grief and anger. She had sacrificed so much to side with David—perhaps even the trust of her father. Maybe in some part of her heart she thought that if David had just stayed a shepherd, none of this would have happened: her father's madness and death, her brother Jonathan's destruction, the fall of the house of Saul. Michal's feelings must have been deep and complicated.

When David returned home to bless his household, Michal daughter of Saul came out to meet him and said, "How the king of Israel has distinguished himself today, going around half-naked in full view of the slave girls of his servants as any vulgar fellow would!"

David said to Michal, "It was before the LORD, who chose me rather than your father or anyone from his house when he appointed me ruler over the LORD's people Israel—I will celebrate before the LORD. I will become even more undignified than this, and I will be humiliated in my own eyes. But by these slave girls you spoke of, I will be held in honor."

And Michal daughter of Saul had no children to the day of her death. (2 Samuel 6:20-23)

What a toxic stew of resentment had brewed in Michal's heart. Her father used her, and it appears the man she once loved was willing to treat her as a political pawn as well. She lashed out at David and he saw right to the heart of what Michal was really getting at: the contrast between her own family and him. David reminded Michal that he was in fact the chosen of the Lord, not her father or her family. If we had any doubts about the state of relations between the two, it appears there was no reconciliation in the cards. Scholars differ on why Michal was childless—whether it was because she and David were never intimate again as husband and wife, or whether God withheld children from her as some form of judgment. In any case, that childlessness meant no descendant of Saul could ever be heir to the throne of King David.

Our marriages do not exist in vacuums. As women, so often we're torn along these very same lines: love for our birth family and loyalty to our new family. That can spark misunderstandings, hurt, and suspicion. For Michal, it gave birth to a lifetime of pain, confusion, and resentment. It all started with a selfish, ego-driven father who never seemed capable of cherishing and protecting his own daughter. That may be the reality for some of you reading these words. It's difficult to trust that our heavenly Father is completely different from the flawed human beings who've been our earthly parents, but He is. If you haven't had a father who modeled trust and acceptance to you, there is healing in God's unwavering love and grace. He knows we are all flawed and that we can deeply wound each other, especially when there's a broken sense of security. God does not guarantee us a Hallmark Channel life (oh how I wish He would!), but He always gives us his presence. We find that in prayer, and it's also right in the pages of the Bible—full of real people with difficult struggles who find peace under their heavenly Father's wings if they choose to rest there.

Lord God, grant us the strength to see You in the clashes and conflicts within our own families and in our own failures. When we are caught between people who dislike or don't trust each other give us the strength to choose love. Help us to show love to those who seem incapable of giving it. Guide us to the truth of Your never-failing presence in our lives. Please bless our own complicated families in all their struggles, and when conflicts arise, grant us the courage and wisdom to face those conflicts with You at our side and in our hearts.

Michal Study Questions
---

1. How poisonous was Saul's jealousy over David? What does it say about him as a father that Saul was more than willing to use his own daughters to try to destroy David? How difficult must it have been for Michal to be caught between her husband and her father? Have you experienced family conflict that stretched your loyalties? How did you resolve it, or are you managing it to keep the peace?

2. How did Saul's plans to use Michal backfire? (1 Samuel 18:28–30)

3. How did Michal try to play both sides of this potentially murderous family conflict? (1 Samuel 19:11–17)

4. How do you imagine Michal must have felt when Saul upended her life again? (1 Samuel 25:44) How did Saul's selfishness and paranoia end up impacting lives far beyond his own?

5. Is David just as guilty of selfishly using Michal, as her father had, without regard to her feelings or wishes? (2 Samuel 3:13)

6. How did bitterness destroy Michal? (2 Samuel 6:20–23) Can we blame her? How can we prevent the seeds of resentment from rooting in our own lives when we've been treated badly?

Miracles for Mothers . . . and Daughters Too

(1 Kings 16:29–33, 1 Kings 17:1, 7–24, 1 Kings 18:17–18,
2 Kings 4:1–7, Mark 5:22–43)

God is never unaware of our struggles, and He is moved by compassion. We see that truth over and over again in both the Old and New Testaments. We should be encouraged by His unlimited supply of grace and mercy for His children. All throughout Scripture, there are stories of God's willingness to step into human heartbreak and turn it to rejoicing. He transforms suffering into purpose and sorrow into joy.

Some of the most beautiful, encouraging moments in the Bible come when we see God reach into the lives of people in the depths of their need. It's a picture that points us to the reality that He is still working in our lives all these centuries later. The stories take us into moments of grief and places where there seemed to be no hope—where we can watch as God delivers a miracle. In our current environment of tumult and uncertainty, who doesn't need that reminder? I know I do, and it's why I take such inspiration and courage in studying the journeys of these mothers and daughters and seeing the deeply compassionate heart of our heavenly Father, who met each of their needs with a miracle. Over and over, we see it was faith that paved the way for divine intervention.

MIRACLES FOR MOTHERS

A pair of Old Testament prophets offers the perfect illustration of how God showed up for two widows in desperate need. Elijah came first to the people of Israel, followed later by his protégé, Elisha. Each was the vehicle for God's miracles to women in crisis. When we meet Elijah, Israel is once again floundering under the leadership of yet another ungodly king.

> In the thirty-eighth year of Asa king of Judah, Ahab son of Omri became king of Israel, and he reigned in Samaria over Israel twenty-two years. Ahab son of Omri did more evil in the eyes of the LORD than any of those before him. He not only considered it trivial to commit the sins of Jeroboam son of Nebat, but he also married Jezebel daughter of Ethbaal king of the Sidonians, and began to serve Baal and worship him. He set up an altar for Baal in the temple of Baal that he built in Samaria. Ahab also made an Asherah pole and did more to arouse the anger of the LORD, the God of Israel, than did all the kings of Israel before him. (1 Kings 16:29–33)

King Ahab was choosing idolatry and wickedness in direct conflict with God's commands for His people. Ahab married Jezebel, a woman who worshipped the pagan god Baal, and then he embraced the abominable practice himself. He also built a temple to Baal for the people of Israel to join in the blasphemous worship. Ahab not only failed to guide the Israelites in the path of righteousness, but the corrupt king actually led the people directly to a false god. God sent Elijah to announce His judgment.

> Now Elijah the Tishbite, from Tishbe in Gilead, said to Ahab, "As the LORD, the God of Israel, lives, whom I serve, there will be neither dew nor rain in the next few years except at my word." (1 Kings 17:1)

In Luke 4:25, we learn this drought lasted three and a half years and led to "severe famine" across the land. During much of this time, Elijah was on the run because Ahab blamed him for the drought and wanted him dead. When these two men met face-to-face three years into the crisis, Ahab pointed his finger at Elijah, and the prophet gave the king a dose of straight talk.

> When [Ahab] saw Elijah, he said to him, "Is that you, you troubler of Israel?"
> "I have not made trouble for Israel," Elijah replied. "But you and your father's family have. You have abandoned the LORD's commands and have followed the Baals." (1 Kings 18:17–18)

Elijah made clear that the pain Israel was experiencing was a direct result of Ahab's sin of worshipping false gods. There was an epic showdown that followed, in which God revealed Himself to the people of Israel in a dramatic way, but tucked inside this blockbuster is the quiet story of a widow and single mother at the end of her rope.

During the time of crushing famine, and before his confrontation with Ahab, God directed Elijah to head to the town of Zarephath, a town that served as a center for Baal worship. The Lord told His prophet that he would meet a widow there who would provide for him. So Elijah headed to the town and happened upon a woman who was gathering sticks. Keep in mind that, during that time, widows were exceptionally vulnerable if they had no male provider in what was a mostly agrarian economy. Elijah began his conversation with the woman by asking her for the one thing that was in incredibly short supply at that time: water.

> "Would you bring me a little water in a jar so I may have a drink?" As she was going to get it, he called, "And bring me, please, a piece of bread." (1 Kings 17:10)

The widow, who was a Gentile, didn't hesitate to go in search of some water for this unknown traveler, but his request didn't stop there. Elijah also asked for something to eat. Yet everyone in the land was desperate for food, including this widow.

> "As surely as the LORD your God lives," she replied, "I don't have any bread—only a handful of flour in a jar and a little olive oil in a jug. I am gathering a few sticks to take home and make a meal for myself and my son, that we may eat it—and die." (1 Kings 17:12)

The woman had no way to know she was part of God's plan for sustaining Elijah at this point, but she did know just how dire her personal circumstances were. She laid it out for Elijah without sugarcoating the reality. *I'm going to use what I have for a last meal and then my son and I are going to perish.* This mother had the same concern any mother would have: giving away the very last of the resources she had to sustain her son's life, however briefly. Had she thought through how these final morsels with her son would taste, knowing it was the end for them? Suddenly a stranger was on the scene asking that she abandon her plan in order to meet his needs.

But Elijah knew God was working, and he quickly reassured the widow.

> Elijah said to her, "Don't be afraid. Go home and do as you have said. But first make a small loaf of bread for me from what you have and bring it to me, and then make something for yourself and your son. For this is what the LORD, the God of Israel, says: 'The jar of flour will not be used up and the jug of oil will not run dry until the day the LORD sends rain on the land.'" (1 Kings 17:13–14)

Elijah made this desperate mother a promise she had no idea if he'd be able to keep. He would have to be a legitimate prophet and miracle worker for any of this to come true. Elijah was asking her to step out in faith. Even though she did not know Elijah's God, He was about to show up for her in a very real way. Notice Elijah was saying to her: *Make me something to eat first. Then, you're free to make a meal for you and your son.* How many times have you found yourself in a similar situation—your resources are limited, but God is calling you to act? Do you struggle to trust in His plans when you can't see the end result?

I cannot tell you how many times I've seen my mom model this. We didn't have much when I was growing up, yet she always found the resources to bless others: taking someone a meal, donating to a missionary raising support, finding a way to work volunteer tutoring into her already jam-packed schedule. If my mom felt moved by the Lord to meet someone else's need, I never saw her hesitate or question how God would make up the deficit. I have no doubt that if my mom was the widow in this story, that bread for Elijah would have been made pronto! By the way, her homemade bread is one of the most delicious things you will ever taste, so be sure she knows you need a loaf.

The widowed mother in Zarephath was just as faithful.

She went away and did as Elijah had told her. (1 Kings 17:15)

Guess what? God is infinitely more faithful than we could ever be, and what Elijah pledged to that desperate mother came to fruition.

So there was food every day for Elijah and for the woman and her family. For the jar of flour was not used up and the jug of oil did not run dry, in keeping with the word of the LORD spoken by Elijah. (1 Kings 17:15–16)

Here the entire region was gripped by crippling famine and starvation, but the faith and sacrifice of a mother wound up providing everything she and her son needed until God lifted His hand of judgment from Israel—three and a half years!

God's provision for this mother in need wasn't over yet. We're told in 1 Kings 17:17 that her son later became very ill.

He grew worse and worse, and finally stopped breathing. She said to Elijah, "What do you have against me, man of

God? Did you come to remind me of my sin and kill my son?" (1 Kings 17:17–18)

My first reaction to this passage was, "You've seen the miracles of Elijah's God, saving both you and your son, and now you're accusing him of this?" Then I remembered: I myself have seen God's provision and intervention, and I have also panicked in the face of tragedy. Our faith is imperfect at times, but God is faithful regardless.

"Give me your son," Elijah replied. He took him from her arms, carried him to the upper room where he was staying, and laid him on his bed. Then he cried out to the LORD, "LORD my God, have you brought tragedy even on this widow I am staying with, by causing her son to die?" Then he stretched himself out on the boy three times and cried out to the LORD, "LORD my God, let this boy's life return to him!"

The LORD heard Elijah's cry, and the boy's life returned to him, and he lived. Elijah picked up the child and carried him down from the room into the house. He gave him to his mother and said, "Look, your son is alive!"

Then the woman said to Elijah, "Now I know that you are a man of God and that the word of the LORD from your mouth is the truth." (1 Kings 17:19–24)

I can't condemn this woman for doubting when I've done it myself. She must have been in great despair, and God heard Elijah's powerful cries on her behalf. Remember, she referred to God as "your God" (1 Kings 17:12) when they first met. By the end of her story, this mother was no longer keeping God at arm's length. Her language shifted; she believed.

Elijah's successor, Elisha, was also a conduit for God's mercy on a struggling mother during his time of prophecy and ministry. This widow had been the wife of a prophet as well and she cried out to Elisha for help when it appeared she was about to lose her sons too.

> "Your servant my husband is dead, and you know that he revered the LORD. But now his creditor is coming to take my two boys as his slaves." Elisha replied to her, "How can I help you? Tell me, what do you have in your house?" "Your servant has nothing there at all," she said, "except a small jar of olive oil." (2 Kings 4:1-2)

This woman had been left with no male provider or protector, and she was about to have her sons stripped away from her as well. Elisha saw this distraught mother's plight and immediately launched into action. He began by asking her how he could help her. I think that is one of the most important questions we can utter when someone is in crisis. Meaning well, we often default to saying, "Just let me know if I can help." But by directly asking this mother to tell him how he could make things better for her, Elisha let her know he was about helping her find a concrete solution.

The widow had nothing to offer to the effort, other than a little bit of olive oil. That, plus her faith, wound up being more than enough. God will never ask more of us than we have to give. Throughout the Bible we see how He multiplied what humans offered to Him. He created everything we know (and more!) out of nothing. He doesn't *need* what we have. What He wants is our faith. In every one of the stories in this chapter, faith and trust precede the miracle God delivers. It's the key ingredient that only we can offer.

The prophet prepared them both for a miracle.

Elisha said, "Go around and ask all your neighbors for empty jars. Don't ask for just a few. Then go inside and shut the door behind you and your sons. Pour oil into all the jars, and as each is filled, put it to one side." (2 Kings 4:3–4)

This wondrous, supernatural provision was going to be a community effort. This frantic mother, herself once married to a prophet like Elisha, knew the power of his words and didn't hesitate to follow his directions.

She left him and shut the door behind her and her sons. They brought the jars to her and she kept pouring. When all the jars were full, she said to her son, "Bring me another one."

But he replied, "There is not a jar left." Then the oil stopped flowing.

She went and told the man of God, and he said, "Go, sell the oil and pay your debts. You and your sons can live on what is left." (2 Kings 4:5–7)

What a story this mother had to tell! Frightened and with virtually no options left for her family, she cried out for help. I love that the miracle God delivered through Elisha wasn't just isolated to this widow and her two sons. It involved everyone who knew their plight and was willing to hand over a jug or container for the oil-collecting endeavor. The widow anticipated divine deliverance, and she communicated that to everyone else by collecting all those vessels. She was then able to testify to each and every one of them as she returned their vessels empty, having sold the oil they miraculously contained at one point.

I don't know about you, but I love rejoicing in seeing someone else's suffering turn into joy, their need into a solution, and their deficit into abundance. We rarely know exactly how God is going to work in any given situation, but we will never be wrong if we go to Him and ask Him for help. Occasionally, God's answer to our prayers comes in the way we hope. More often the resolution arrives via an unexpected path, but always in a way that grows our faith and gives God the glory. The brightest examples of hope in my life right now are people who are walking through dark valleys. Their reliance on God and deliberate choice to dig their foundations even deeper into His promises, despite their circumstances, is both a challenge and an inspiration to me. I pray that, just as He was in the stories of these obedient widowed mothers, God will be so clearly evident in my friends' journeys.

Centuries ago, and in many places still today, widows were incredibly vulnerable without a husband to protect and provide for them. All throughout the Bible, God makes clear that we are to care for mothers in distress.

Do not take advantage of the widow or the fatherless. (Exodus 22:22)

A father to the fatherless, a defender of widows,
   is God in his holy dwelling. (Psalm 68:5)

Give proper recognition to those widows who are really in
need. (1 Timothy 5:3)

Religion that God our Father accepts as pure and faultless
is this: to look after orphans and widows in their distress.
(James 1:27)

These priorities are perfectly illustrated in the story of the
widow of Nain in Luke 7. When Jesus encountered her, this
woman had not only lost her husband but was also walking in the
funeral procession for her own son. The Bible tells us Jesus's heart
broke for this woman and He immediately brought her son back
to life (Luke 7:14–15). There was enormous rejoicing that also led
to the spread of the Gospel message throughout the region (Luke
7:17). May we also be His instrument to mothers in need. That
can show up in countless ways from carpools to casseroles. If you
sense God leading you to reach out, follow His prompts. Trust
me, you'll both end up blessed!

MIRACLES FOR DAUGHTERS

The Gospels also bring us the story of a daughter (or two) in need
of a miracle. The initial request for help came during the period
in Jesus's ministry when word of His healings and supernatural
power was spreading far and wide. That often meant He was sur-
rounded by crowds, pressing on him literally and figuratively.
It's amid one of these masses of people that we see a father's frantic plea for his daughter.

> Then one of the synagogue leaders, named Jairus, came, and when he saw Jesus, he fell at his feet. He pleaded earnestly with him, "My little daughter is dying. Please come and put your hands on her so that she will be healed and live." (Mark 5:22-23)

Who was this man begging Jesus to help him? Well, we know Jairus was a man in a position of power. Not only that, but Jairus was a religious leader. Remember, many of the religious leaders in Jesus's day did not believe He was divine or sent by God the Father. In fact, they thought Jesus was a heretic and wanted to shut Him up. Jairus had apparently become convinced otherwise, or else he was so desperate to save his daughter that he was willing to humble himself before Jesus and take a chance. In either case, he took action on behalf of his beloved daughter, who was dying.

Amid the throngs of people gathered around Jesus that day, this elevated religious dignitary literally threw himself at Jesus's feet. Jairus wasn't worried about impressing the crowds that were pressing in on Jesus. Jairus wasn't trying to save face or distance himself from this controversial man who made astounding claims. With his precious daughter close to death, Jairus humbled himself and showed faith that Jesus could save her simply by putting His hands on her. No doubt there were countless other people asking Him for help, but Jesus immediately responded to the unpretentious, direct request of a man who may have been risking his own position in order to save his daughter.

> So Jesus went with him. A large crowd followed and pressed around him. (Mark 5:24)

Imagine how Jairus must have felt, flooded with enormous hope! Time was of the essence, yet Jairus had been able not only to get to Jesus, but also to convince Him to rush to his dying daughter's bedside. Not so fast.

With the clock ticking, Jesus hit a detour. It's a story I've visited many times before—and one of my favorites. A woman who'd been suffering with an "issue of bleeding" for twelve years was desperate for help. No one had been able to cure her. In fact, she'd only gotten worse. Plus, she'd spent every penny she had looking for a solution. She'd heard of Jesus and decided if she could just touch the hem of His garment that would be enough to heal her. This wasn't without risk, though. According to Old Testament law, this continuous bleeding would have made her ceremonially unclean, meaning she shouldn't have been around other people. Like Jairus, she humbled herself and took her case straight to the One she believed could make her whole.

This woman's miraculous healing did happen with her simple touch of Jesus's cloak. He knew it, and she knew it. When he turned around and asked who'd touched Him, the woman fell down before him in fear and trembling and "told him the whole truth" (Mark 5:33). Jesus would have had every right to chastise or berate her, but He did exactly the opposite. In every account in the Gospels, the first thing He did was address her with the tender word *daughter* (Matthew 9:22; Mark 5:34; Luke 8:48), and then He credited her faith as the source of her healing.

We have no idea how long this interaction took. Exactly how much of her twelve years of sorrow and despair did this woman pour out when she was sharing her "whole truth" with Jesus? There was a distraught father standing by, a respected synagogue leader waiting to whisk Jesus straight to his dying daughter, yet Christ chose to interact with this woman many in the crowd probably viewed as a rule-breaking distraction. Even in light of the emergency with Jairus's daughter, Jesus was purposeful in stopping to see a "daughter" of His own. He is never too busy for us, and He knows our suffering. The Bible tells us that by coming to earth, Christ experienced all our human frailties, yet without sin.

> **For we do not have a high priest who is unable to empathize with our weaknesses. (Hebrews 4:15)**

God isn't too busy to handle multiple crises at a time, as that crowd was about to discover.

Not everyone could see Jesus's divine plan, though, and the update from Jairus's home was crushing.

> **While Jesus was still speaking, some people came from the house of Jairus, the synagogue leader. "Your daughter is dead," they said. "Why bother the teacher anymore?" Overhearing what they said, Jesus told him, "Don't be afraid; just believe." (Mark 5:35–36)**

There was clearly a limit to what the people who came from Jairus's house were willing to believe about Jesus. But what about Jairus, the religious leader? He'd already made clear he thought Jesus could lay hands on his daughter and heal her, but what about raising her from the dead? Before we can find out what this grieving father must have been thinking, Jesus told him to reject fear and embrace faith.

We will all have shocking moments in life: a heartbreaking phone call, an unexpected loss, news that shakes our deepest foundations. It's natural for us, as fallible human beings, to react in panic or doubt. Jesus asks us to cast away both options. Sometimes it's as simple as a whispered prayer: *"Lord, I can't handle this. Please help me."* It doesn't have to be poetic or fancy. He knows our hearts and the struggles we're wrestling with. Jesus was direct with Jairus—*Don't let fear creep in; keep believing in Me.* That must be what Jairus did, because he didn't say, *"No, it's too late. I shouldn't waste any more of Your time."* Instead, they went straight to his daughter's bedside.

Jesus took only His closest companions inside Jairus's house, and they found what you'd expect at the home of a young girl who had just died.

> **Jesus saw a commotion, with people crying and wailing loudly. He went in and said to them, "Why all this commotion and wailing? The child is not dead but asleep." But they laughed at him. After he put them all out, he took the child's father and mother and the disciples who were with him, and went in where the child was. (Mark 5:38–41)**

The mourning was underway, but Jesus knew what was coming. He would soon escape death Himself; it had no power over Him. Whether He was waking up someone from a nap or raising them from the dead, both were equally possible for Jesus. Yet when He suggested the girl would be fine, those sobs turned to laughter. Was it an expression of disbelief or mocking? In any case, God is not unfamiliar with doubting humans who chuckle over His miraculous plans.

Remember Abraham and Sarah and their reaction when God told them they'd have a son at an extremely advanced age?

> Abraham fell facedown; he laughed and said to himself, "Will a son be born to a man a hundred years old? Will Sarah bear a child at the age of ninety?" (Genesis 17:17)

> So Sarah laughed to herself as she thought, "After I am worn out and my lord is old, will I now have this pleasure?" Then the LORD said to Abraham, "Why did Sarah laugh and say, 'Will I really have a child, now that I am old?' Is anything too hard for the LORD? I will return to you at the appointed time next year, and Sarah will have a son."
> Sarah was afraid, so she lied and said, "I did not laugh." But he said, "Yes, you did laugh." (Genesis 18:12–15)

Just as God called out Sarah for trying to hide her faithless reaction to His promise, Jesus told the skeptical mourners at Jairus's home to get out. I love how direct Jesus was in this story; the Bible tells us He "put them all out" (Matthew 5:40). He wasn't having it. Jesus was about His Father's business.

> He took her by the hand and said to her, *"Talitha koum!"* (which means "Little girl, I say to you, get up!"). Immediately the girl stood up and began to walk around (she was twelve years old). At this they were completely astonished. (Mark 5:41–42)

In a single passage, Jesus had healed two daughters in desperate need. In both cases, faith preceded the miracles. I also believe both cases turned deep suffering into glorious testimonies to the truth of who Jesus Christ was—and is. I often think about the woman who had suffered so much with her crippling illness, and how her entire life would become proof of Jesus's divinity as she shared her story. And what about Jairus? He was a leader in the synagogue, a place where there were not just doubters but also outright enemies of Jesus. Jairus would be able to tell them face-to-face about the miracle he'd witnessed from Jesus. As we saw Christ do following other miracles He'd performed, Mark 5:43 tells us He gave everyone who witnessed the resurrection of Jairus's daughter "strict orders" not to tell anyone else. Did they obey? The leper Jesus healed in Mark 1:42 sure didn't follow those orders.

> Instead he went out and began to talk freely, spreading the news. As a result, Jesus could no longer enter a town openly but stayed outside in lonely places. Yet the people still came to him from everywhere. (Mark 1:45)

Was Jesus concerned that word of His miracles would detract from the more important underlying mission He was on: to seek and to save the lost (Luke 19:10)? Miracles were certainly part of His ministry, and we often read that Jesus was moved with compassion for those He encountered who were despondent and hopeless (Matthew 9:36). But if the crowds were only interested in seeing Jesus do "magic tricks," then there was a danger they'd miss the real message.

Jesus was sent to redeem us all, not just show up as a good luck charm when we need Him. God is driven by compassion not only to meet our physical, earthly needs, but He's also about delivering an even bigger gift: salvation. Sometimes the growth He knows we need comes as the result of pruning we likely don't want. There is purpose in all of it. As in the stories of these mothers and daughters who received miracles, their faith was strengthened and God was glorified.

Lord, give us the courage to reject fear and to cling to You when life is uncertain and difficult. Help us to step forward in faith when You direct us to trust and believe. Grant us the ability to turn away from doubt and doubters, when they call us to question Your goodness and Your plans. Remind us that while life will not be without suffering, You are always working in the seasons of struggle. Help us to remember to turn to You every day, not only when we are in peril. May we tend to our relationship with You through every season.

Miracles for Mothers . . . and Daughters Too
Study Questions

---

1. What role did faith play in the miracles in this chapter?

2. What did Jairus risk in throwing himself before Jesus for help?

3. Have you felt compelled to obey God when it didn't make sense? Have you found yourself doubting, even when you've seen God work in the past? How did you overcome any hesitation or learn from the trial? What does God tell us about confronting fear? (Mark 5:36)

4. How did Jesus react to those who mocked or displayed disbelief? (Mark 5:40) How can His reaction guide the way we respond to those who question our faith?

5. How can you see in these stories that a delay in response to a request for help wound up serving a greater purpose?

ACKNOWLEDGMENTS

The pages of this book bear the inspiration and work of scores of talented, dedicated people who guided it from dream to reality. From my earliest Sunday School teachers at First Baptist Church of West Hollywood to the wise theologians across the country I rely on for guidance today, thank you for pouring your knowledge into this earthen vessel. All glory to my Heavenly Father for making sure these women's stories wound up in the Bible, and for directing my path to cross with those who help me share them.

Jennifer Stair, your insights and encouragement made every chapter better and the process much more joyful. Mary Grace DuPree, your acumen made these women more accessible and their life lessons even more valuable. Hannah Long, you are brilliant and sharp; what a privilege it is to work alongside you.

Michael Tammero, you are our secret weapon in so many ways. Your upbeat attitude, endless messaging ideas, and passion to make sure Fox News Books connects with people around the world is unmatched. I am humbly grateful to be a part of the team!

None of what I do in life could ever be accomplished without God's greatest earthly gift to me, Sheldon. Thank you for being the unwavering rock in my life for nearly thirty years. Every struggle is more manageable, every victory is sweeter, every adventure is exponentially more fun because of you.

Momma, you've been praying for me since long before I ever arrived. You planted God's Word deep in my heart from an early age and continue to model His grace, forgiveness and love in human form. Thank you for covering me, and this book, in constant prayer.

I cannot adequately express the depths to which I feel blessed every time someone, stranger or friend, says to me, "I'm praying for you." My wholehearted appreciation to those who often remind me: Magen, Debbie, Penny, Lynne, Angie, Sarah, Molly, Anna, Charlie, Pastor Jeffress, Greg and Cathe, the Sorority and the Coraggios. To Olivia, thank you for helping me to realize so many dreams—including ones I didn't know I had! Tessa, I'd be a mess without you. Your sunny disposition, hard work, deep faith, and cutting-edge dance moves make life more fun! And to the *Fox News @ Night* team: I'd never be able to juggle doing these things I love without your dedication, excellence, and understanding.

Joel Rosenberg and Karen Kinsbury, I deeply admire you both as authors and friends. Your guidance and encouragement have been a blessing, and often just the gust of wind that I needed to keep moving in the right direction.

Kathy Progar, as you walk through the most challenging season of your life, your transparency and witness have been a beacon to me—a real life example of what it means to cling to, and celebrate, God's promises when circumstances test the very foundations of your faith.

ABOUT THE AUTHOR

SHANNON BREAM is the author of the number one *New York Times* bestseller *The Women of the Bible Speak,* the anchor of *Fox News @ Night,* and the chief legal correspondent for Fox News Channel. She has covered landmark cases at the Supreme Court and heated political campaigns and policy battles from the White House to Capitol Hill.